THE NEW ASTROLOGY

Poppé Folly

THE NEW ASTROLOGY

A Pan Original
Pan Books London and Sydney

First published 1985 by Pan Books Ltd
Cavaye Place London SW10 9PG
9 8 7 6 5 4 3 2 1

ISBN 0 330 29084 3

Printed and bound in Great Britain by
Richard Clay (The Chaucer Press) Ltd, Bungay, Suffolk

CONTENTS

INTRODUCTION

We live in an age of shrinking budgets, government cuts and shortening tempers. You can shoot a man in a traffic jam and plead justifiable homicide. You can murder your wife and survive the retrial. It is a disturbing world, where reassurance is sought, but is not genuinely believed, where flattery is preferred, but counter-productive.

In the early Middle Ages, there was a limited concept of market forces. Villeins had complete job security. You could not fire a villein for indolence, any more than a villein could be drawn by a more attractive package in a neighbouring barony. Thus, Libran skills (communication, mobility, diplomacy) were of small commercial value.

In this great but terrible world we inhabit, of food processors, of word processors, beauty consultants, telephone cleaners, off-shore money, single-parent families, cocaine dealers, tax planners, trust lawyers, cable TV, sit-coms, electronic cottages, and the mass supply of ten-speed bicycles, Piscean skills are at a discount – even though we still live in the Age of Pisces.

Piscean skills (religious aptitude, low consumer-expectations, the capacity to withstand pain on the soles of your feet as they are beaten with proto-teaspoons) are helpful to no one but workers in heavy industry. It is Libran skills that are prized, which include (conventional astrologers would demur at this) an appalling certainty that you are right (Mrs Thatcher is a Libran).

Is Astrology True?

We astrologers believe astrology to be a psychic diagram of the objective interconnectedness of many worlds. We believe it expresses the fundamental wholeness of the cosmos, the idea that everything is implicit in everything else, that we can see in the stars as much as can be seen in a grain of sand: we can see everything, everything; the entire universe (except perhaps the money supply). Astrologers know this to be true. But they don't know whether it is any use.

Does Astrology Actually Work?

Diagnostic astrology ('What's my star sign, you ought to know, you're an astrologer?') is a slut of a business.

Diagnose this man: he's 32 and a lawyer. He gets drunk and quarrels about the importance of sorting out his karma. He eats one really hot curry a week to clean the blood (this is why he has no pimples): he remembers to sleep with his mouth open after drinking (this is why he's never had a hangover in his life).

Was this man born under a) Taurus (his slow monotonous voice indicates how he will finish a sentence almost before he has started it); b) Aries (if you contradict him long enough he will eventually punch you); c) Capricorn (he will never give up his point of view); or d) Pisces (*everything* he believes – telepathic dolphins, the electromagnetism of reincarnation, the insemination of apes 300,000 years ago by spacemen – is drivel)? He could be a Libran trying to annoy you, or a drunk Sagittarian. He could be a rare Virgoan with a sense of mischief. Were it not for the violence he could be an Aquarian (I've never seen him punch someone, but he's only 32).

The fact is, astrology finds it difficult to predict anything. A page of horoscopes has the same validity as the Rorschach Test, a psychological examination in which you may discern from a page of ink blobs some sort of picture, some pattern. In a page of astrology you may glimpse the outline of a character, a flash of personality, however unwelcome. Statistics may be used to discredit this practice, but in the opinion of this astrologer any attempt to make sense of the moving shadows of impulse, instinct, appetite and fear is well spent.

ARIES
(20 March – 20 April)

You Ariens are the most spiritually immature member of the Zodiac, and consequently the one with the greatest hunger for admiration. Some examples (Rolf Harris, Michael Parkinson) have a curious way of going about it, though others (the late Marshal of the RAF Sir Arthur 'Bomber' Harris) don't go about it at all.

The Karma

Your impossible mission in this life is to grow up. Your soul has chosen the April incarnation to learn how little 'I want' delivers; to learn the emptiness of material desires; to learn that the worst thing for the ambitious is to achieve their ambition. For this reason the Aries personality suffers from chronic over-achievement: you will not rest without experiencing this Queen Anne house, that kilo of cocaine, those girls in strange uniforms who leave you gasping on the carpet. Of everything you have you want more. It is a deep neurosis, particularly obvious in matters of money. Sir Alec Guinness complains about being short of money *even though he had points in the gross of Star Wars*!

Astrological Opposition

Aries in the First House is naturally opposed to Libra in the Seventh House.

The Seventh House is that of harmony, partnership, marital pleasures, mutual cooperation and compromise. The First House is that of throwing javelins at people (not necessarily people you don't like, either).

However, despite the wildness of the sign, and despite the fact that April Fool's Day falls within it, there are surprisingly few outright idiots born under Aries. Except Paul Gambaccini.

The Arien Personality

Ariens lead school demonstrations and the drunk-driving statistics. Your cross-body coshwork is the maturest thing about you. Those caught up in the local disturbance of your personality may be so close to the brutal emotional scenes surrounding you (Tennesee Williams, Lucrezia Borgia) that they take you on your own terms, but disappointment inevitably follows. Your greatest Arien trait is to promise more than you deliver, and consequently – viz. Ariens Kinnock, Tebbit, Benn, Steel and Ian Paisley – you rarely achieve high office. Papa Doc Duvalier was an interesting exception to this rule, but Caribbean politics offer a more Arien interpretation of electioneering, to include your astrological talent for murder and sexual assault by enormous negroes. It is true that Arien Mrs Bandaranaike achieved office as a prime minister, but then it was only Sri Lanka she was prime minister of.

You Ariens would be fascists if you were community minded, but you don't fit in with other peoples' plans as proper fascists are keen to do. You are generally too fast, too furious, too quick with your fists. You are mavericks, madmen, satirists. Your penetrating, wide-ranging eye is usually directed over other peoples' shoulders looking for someone more interesting to talk to, someone who can better help your career. You really do want to be popular, but this kind of behaviour does not make it easy for you. But Bismarck was an Arien, so there you are.

You have a real need to be the cleverest boy in the school (Aries prototype Malcolm Muggeridge is over 80 and still needs it). This early failure is often the first and deepest of your resentments. However, you take it out in the scrum (*'Trample!'*), where you excel. Latterly you prefer playing games that have violent physical contact and absolutely no rules, like Gaelic football.

It is this tendency that makes a mess of your tax situation. You despise tax avoidance. Real men simply don't pay tax, they tough it out, sending contemptuous and insulting letters to their inspector, and when the going gets too hot they move to Saudi Arabia on a three-year contract. So do you, your worst career move.

Minor Reservations

In your Aries mode you are utterly self-absorbed, and yet quite uninterested in yourself as a subject for enquiry. You are a mechanism for processing self-gratification. If you can suck it, snort it, drink it, or drive it at 140 m.p.h. into Calabria with a naked blonde in the passenger seat you will be interested. If not, not. You do not care to look too closely into motives, and with a character like yours this is not surprising.

The tangible, material, physical world is your only way of understanding. You like books with big pictures. And short sentences. Like this. And this. Except sub-titles. You hate sub-titles so much you haven't seen a foreign film since 1975. Not even *Diva*.

Arien Invectives

Ariens are notorious in the Zodiac for their foul mouths. Mary Pickford, affectionately known as 'The World's Sweetheart', at one time had the foulest mouth in Hollywood. She used to shout bizarre insults at strangers admiring her home from beyond the perimeter fence. 'Get a big black dog up your ass!' was her most common piece of invective, followed by 'Go on John, get that black animal up your anus!'

Aries And Their Penile Symbols

This is the sign of driving around in MGBs, of gunning engines and squealing tyres. You lob your keys to parking attendants (or passers-by who look like parking attendants). You pick street fights with people who are walking too slowly in front of you. You nudge stroppy little Fiats under flatboards carrying scaffolding rods, and this appeals to what you call your sense of humour. You carve up traffic, braking in front of motoring offenders, getting out of your car to insult them, possibly in extreme cases to let down their tyres. You believe in capital punishment, particularly for those who enter a yellow box junction without being able to get out. The Arien has a very quick clutch – when you spring it, your over-revved engine snatches *dangerously* at the gearing and the whole chassis shudders.

Relentless Self-Publicists

Jeffrey Archer is a classic Aries ('The only reason I'm first in the New York list of best sellers and Graham Greene is seventeenth is because I get out there and promote my books and he won't. I can't understand that guy'). And David Frost the Bubonic Plagiarist is as well, along with Renee Descartes, Hugh Hefner, Erik von Daniken, and Bishop Abel Muzorewa. Peter Ustinov has taken the Arien sexual trait of going *on* and *on* and applied it to his social life.

Impulsive, Reckless, Attractive

Ariens liquidate trusts, realize stock maturities, take profits, cash in, flip out. You will do anything to be the centre of attention. And you make popular rich people, though not for long. Algy Cluff may be an Arien exception to this. You hunger for money, you want far too much of it, and you will do anything to get it (sell drugs, take out oil leases, star in suck shows, marry madwomen, *any*thing). You have a talent for speed over thin ice. You enter into litigation with tremendous enthusiasm, ever-conscious of your public face, reputation and dignity (you haven't got any). If poor and inconsequential, you yearn to be libelled, both for the recognition it brings as well as the settlement in damages. Your appetite for glamour is insatiable, and when your appetites fail, you die, often by your own hand in an impulsive, reckless and attractive manner.

The Dangerous Sports Club was instituted under Aries. Interestingly, one of its Arien members was standing on the Clifton Suspension Bridge in 1981 attached to the metal work by a precisely calculated length of elastic. On impulse, and immediately prior to the jump, he added two metres into the line. When he hit the ground he broke every bone in his body. He was in hospital for nine months. His Taurean parents *never came to visit him.*

Ecclesiastes

'Whatever thou doest, do with thy might lest thou come to where there is no knowledge, no device or no desire, in the grave, whither thou art going.' Whatever Ariens do they do to extremes, whether in the matter of corruption (Baudelaire), music (both the Lloyd Webbers), or the screen presentation of public school gutlessness (Michael York). Aries is a sign of neurotic extremity, subject to wild swings of emotion. The fact is you are just deeply unreliable. Spike Milligan's initial philanthropy turns to a yearning for a damn good nuclear war to bring the world to its senses. Werner von Braun, significantly, is his fellow Arien.

Great Campaigners, Prison Warders, Homosexuals

You have a passion for persuading everyone to see things your way, to act as a lens for society. This *monstrous* egotism has, interestingly, produced Dirk Bogarde (*Flower Arranging Was For Sundays*) and Anita Bryant (*Save Our Children From Ghastly Benders*).

In Business

You peak early (Eric Clapton used to be God, Rachmaninov, for all his Slavic genius, died in Beverly Hills, and Hayley Mills made her best film when she was 12). Thus your astrology drives you into breach of contract. Your impulse is to start-up and sell-out in a year. You are a sprinter. You will do all the work, become bored, leave others the rewards. You are always in too much of a hurry to get the best price.

Terrified by your mortality, you will work yourself to death to forget you are going to die. After fifty-three years of frantic engineering Brunel's brain blew up. It went with a sort of dull thud, and so he was no more. The same thing happened to Vivian 'Spend! Spend! Spend!' Nicholson, except she is still alive. Ariens have a lower life expectancy than most (you can't take the heart attacks). You often die at work – the inconvenience to others does not deter you. Strokes, high blood pressure, and ulcerated soft organs will bring about a premature retirement. Everyone is relieved.

Career Path

Impatient of detail, you want to be in on the big picture and this makes you virtually unemployable in your early career. Against this you seem – like Ariens Eric Idle, Stephen Sondheim, Chapman Pincher – to be much more talented than you actually are, and this helps early promotion.

In time Ariens can grow into decisive and talented hatchet men who are capable of firing virtually anyone. You don't care, you just call them into your office and say, 'You're out, Tom, it's too bad, I need you to pack your desk and leave the building within forty-five minutes.' One of your most annoying characteristics is taking charge of a crisis. You do this successfully, particularly when the crisis is of your own devising. You are never more annoying than at this time.

However much you succeed in your company structure, rising above the trail of debts, debris and human wreckage, nonetheless a wise and experienced chairman will never let you into positions of real responsibility. He will gloss over the plots of yours he uncovers, fire the secretaries you have sexually abused, initial the fraudulent expenses you put in, but he knows that deep down you are not spiritually equipped for the jump from sales director to managing director. You lack bottom. You are a maverick, a counter-puncher. No matter how well you do at the top you will sooner or later come unstuck, taking the company into some ruinous diversification, sinking the profits into a wild R and D programme, screwing all the secretaries as a condition of their employment, spending the cash surplus on drugs when depressed, throwing typewriters out of windows when annoyed. You crave freedom, crave the hyper-oxygenated atmosphere of the highest management – but it will poison your brain. You simply don't have the lungs.

The wise chairman will keep the Arien employee down there on a choke chain like a dangerous, useful, Doberman.

Making A Mess Of The Arien In A Board Meeting

The fast, foolish volunteers that Ariens are have fancy footwork, but the speed of their feet can deceive the eye. Often listeners need to be reminded that the feet are travelling in different directions. Preserve your distance from Ariens. You won't be able (or even want) to keep up with their youthful enthusiasm for getting on with things. They will never grow out of being young, pro-active account executives and they never *really* learn. Sooner or later they will give themselves away by hiring a limo to fly the company flags on the bonnet to a client presentation in Macclesfield.

In replying to the Arien, slow your speech by half (his fast, exclamatory manner betrays his lack of experience). A pleasant weariness is effective. Do not tackle him head on. Agree with him, and put leading cases to him, allowing his enthusiasm to draw him into increasingly ridiculous situations. Be silently but expressively regretful when the imbecility of his position becomes clear to everyone. You can go too far. He simply will not be aware of how deeply he has been humiliated.

He needs cooperation and support, but he is the worst in the Zodiac to generate it: his flanks are always exposed; his naked self-interest is a joke. He breaks his bones but he hates the handicapped.

The Aries Library

Win Through Intimidation.

Sexually

The butting, repetitive, penile symbolism with which your sign is loaded suggests an unreconstructed public school attitude to sex. Arien men talk highly competitive pussy in the locker room. So women eventually find you gross. Even gross women find you gross, *Sagittarian* women find you gross.

As spiritual alley men you are sexually adventurous, recklessly so, and you come at girls in a fighter's crouch, often from the first introduction. Your language is direct. You say to anyone: menopausal women, jailbait, frigid Sloanes, incredibly unhygienic Irishwomen (you're a sexual democrat), 'Take your clothes off, *quickly*, if I don't have you I'll *die*!' You grip them quickly in cocktail bars, never at a loss for something to fill the silence – a joke, or a part of your body. You take them home for a coffee and strip them on the carpet, often in the hall. There is never any question you will succeed. Your direct approach always cops totty, often ugly totty, but you're a sexual democrat and you do not care.

A woman's personality, her needs and fears do not interest you. It is connected with your need to have everyone acquiesce in your world view. Your view of people as objects. In some obscure way you want everything to die.

However, alone in the Zodiac, you Arien men are confident your sexual dimensions are fully adequate. You have the certainty, the quite unfounded certainty, that women find you irresistable. Consequently you generally are. You are vigorous and inventive in bed, spontaneous in the back of your Bentley, or between floors in a stranded elevator. It is your luck that women are fatally attracted to almost anyone who genuinely (though not desperately) wants to see them naked.

Women like your excited brainlessness – they can relax in the presence of your naked self-interest. Faced with the elevated self-consciousness, balance, harmony of (say) Librans, post-coital women dolefully say 'I feel like a whore'. Your porky performance allows them to say 'I'm a perfectly normal woman with healthy appetites'. Considering what you were doing the night before, this is incredible to anyone except astrologers.

Actually Doing It

In bed you are fiery and unpredictable. No orifice, no crease of flesh even, is immune from your investigations. You probe promiscuously; effectively sometimes and feckless at others (you don't notice the difference). You turn her like a kipper in the pan. However, it must be said that foreplay bores you. The latticework of interconnected caresses is without interest for you, the building rhythm, the feedback and forward thrust are irrelevant – you're simply in there and at her, like a jack-hammer, from the first.

If she whispers 'Talk to me' during the act of love, you do. You let her have it. She gets the works. She doesn't usually ask again. But Aries doesn't need to be asked a second time.

You have read enough to know that the New Man is expected to 'use his mouth' as girls call it, and so you do, to the point of anaesthesia. There is your reputation to consider. You don't mind if she doesn't reciprocate – you feel curiously left out of things, if and while she does.

Your sexual conversation is thematically simple but you make up in vigour what you lack in imagination; though this is no consolation to her as she limps around the office for the next two days. Sexually you have a great deal to say, even if most of it is the same as much of the rest of it. The sexual conversation may often turn into a sexual argument but you usually win (at least in the short term).

Question: What proportion of your bouts of sexual intercourse end successfully for the woman?

Arien: No idea! I do my part!

However, Ariens can be prey to post-coital confusion because sex for them includes *ideals* as well as actions and feelings, and you are liable to disappointment finding out how filthy sex is, at its best. Your idealism can also lead you into mindless promiscuity as you are drawn through life by your willy (something that gets painful towards the end, as Hugh Hefner is even now complaining).

The Arien Climax

You can be prey to premature ejaculation (the over excitement is too much), but as you want to do it again almost immediately this is not serious. You have the climax for both of you.

The climax itself is signalled by a series of little snuffling grunts, like a welterweight being punched in the face. Your expression matches this (not a pretty sight, don't let partners see it without preparing them first).

Sexual Problems

None, except your knuckles bruise easily.

But So Sensitive

Other signs may be surprised that such a positive, aggressive, dynamic person can be demoralized by the simple sight of a woman cutting her toenails over a newspaper, or plucking her legs with a pair of tweezers in front of *The Dukes Of Hazzard.* Your idealized beliefs of what life and love are cannot survive the sight of your wife peeling off a bikini wax. Aries will retreat from these ordinary domestic scenes as if from a gas attack.

What You Want

You need a submissive. Cancerian women often seem to fit the bill. It is not until you marry her that her inner strength (much greater than yours) becomes apparent, and then it is too late. You are a sprinter but she has stamina. The race is not to the swift, but to the one who can wear you down over the years into giving up social rugby, cutting down drink, ironing your own shirts, attending to her problems with her mother.

Alas, for all your violent activity you are curiously weak, depending on (without recognizing) the cooperation of those you have bruised. Every other sign of the Zodiac feels deeply superior to Aries (you hate this more than anything).

Women

Demanding, passionate, reckless, you get pregnant a lot. You are a precautionary tale. You scoff drugs and long for success, but when it comes you have no idea of what to do with it. Your greatest horror is having to settle down, and so you never really do – no matter how happy and comfortable you may be, you always keep an eye on the horizon, an eye on the side door to see who may be coming on stream. Your drive to stand out of the crowd, to have everyone looking at you is probably your father's fault. He never gave you the unconditional love you needed. He didn't dare, for fear of providing you with a stronger personality than you already had. This problem will recur through life – no one will give you the unconditional love you want. No one except large, cheerfully submissive dogs.

You have a terribly *strong* personality, but so strong it makes you stupid: everything is going out and nothing coming in: a yawning intellectual trade deficit: 'Educating the masses is wrong because it gives people too great expectations in life.' If asked to back this up you will say, as if into a hearing aid, '*Because it gives people too great expectations in life.*'

You don't really mind what you say as long as it is listened to, and you pick up information without breaking stride, while you are talking. While others talk you are either trying to catch your breath or thinking what you are going to say next. Very often you don't need to think, you just open your mouth for anything in there to pop out.

Warning To Other Signs

Never interrupt an Arien woman. It is like walking into on-coming traffic.

Nasty But Nice

You Aries women have a need to dominate every situation you walk in on. You stand bossily in the middle of the room, one foot cocked up on its heel, looking for lieutenants. You have a loud voice, and the confidence that you will be heard forms your personality from an early age: but your voice will also degenerate with age and disappointment into a fractured mezzo that makes the family jump. This will reform your personality in your middle years, probably not for the better. However, your abundant energy is attractive to those who don't have to stand too close to you (you can spit). You are at your best at a drinks party where no one expects you to listen. You make impact more than contact, and you would be an indispensable guest if you ever arrived on time to kick start the others into action.

You are endlessly optimistic that everything will turn out all right in the end (it never does, but you don't notice). This, in moderation, is your most attractive feature, though not to anyone else who has to live with you. Because you can be so competitive, stubborn, unyielding, this optimism can take on an aggressive, scornful edge. One of your major talents is facing unpleasant truths. Your major pleasure is in making those close to you face them too. This makes you sensationally unforgiving; a demonic energy is called up when you discover you have been deceived – you are at your most alive when on the point of actual homicide. However, you are never dishonest (except in its deepest sense: you are outstandingly frank but you don't really have the intellectual or emotional apparatus to be really *honest*), and never financially mean (it's why you never have any money of your own).

Forthright Mode Of Speech

You are imperative, captious, astringent in your conversation: '*Oh* get up!' and '*Pull* yourself together!' (Arien Joanna Hemingway's last words to her stepfather). You come into your own in docile crowds where you have no hesitation in saying to a strange man, 'Would you mind not making that disgusting noise with your gums when you swallow, it's making me feel quite ill.'

Other signs should not be offended when you say in reply to one of their unexceptional remarks, '*Oh grow up*!' or 'Don't be p'*thetic*!' Other signs are unable to say what they mean and phrase the same sentiments as 'Well, I'm not sure, I'll have to think about that one before committing myself.'

Conversations with Arien women can often take the form of:

You: I saw a chap and—
Arien: You're sending it to *Japan?*
You: No, I was saying I'd seen a *chap*, and he—
Arien: Oh, send it to *Japan*, I would if I were you. It's a *fabulous* country. I was there in 1978 and *I* thought . . .

Your Career

Start at the top is your dictum, so much so that you often never start at all. Selfish, proud and vain, you are unemployable in any conventional sense, nurturing ideas well beyond your station. You are full of advice for the sales director, the charge hands, the guard dogs.

You are good material for any cause, any campaign – feminism suits you, though you are inclined to treat men not as equals but as objects (actually you are inclined to treat everyone as objects). Your competitive, stubborn, unyielding approach, however, can be invaluable and you never lose your surprise at being surrounded by idiots – what is it? Do you attract idiots? Do you *make* people idiotic? You certainly make things happen, and this, within reason, can be an advantage. You can make fine journalists, hunt saboteurs, and a certain sort of actress (Penelope Keith, for instance) and though your talent for causes may lead you into politics you will never achieve high office.

What you appear to be best at is occupying the centre stage. You need *some* justification for staying there, so many of you start singing. A surprising number of semi-stars – Sarah Vaughan, soprano Margaret Price, Loretta Lynn, Dusty Springfield, Dame Bridget D'Oyly Carte, Radio Caroline, David Cassidy and Simone Signoret are Ariens.

Romantically

You demand more love than you get, for obvious reasons. You snatch at love and miss, invariably fumbling the pass: you can throw but you can't catch.

During the early stages you will argue with anyone who attracts you, and glow with a sexual flush as you do. Your way of bringing yourself to a man's attention is to contradict him with fierce and irrational rudeness. This is how you are cute.

You claim to feel the need for the smack of firm government, but you will only be really happy with an acquiescent man, a matrimonial accessory in some neutral colour to go with your shoes and bags. This is unless he is particularly clever, and more than usually pitiless.

Sexually

Men who like sex like you. You met such a man once in 1976. You feel you have so much to learn that there is very little time to get it all in, and you are therefore susceptible to three-in-a-bed romps (the third party you prefer to be male, if not an obscenely developed woman). You are fast off the mark, and often the first to call a cab after the encounter, and men generally agree this is your most attractive characteristic. When you get under way, the neighbours often call the Flying Squad. You rake, gouge, writhe, show off and *talk* – you are the centre of attention in this as in everything else. You only touch your partner to goad him into ever more vigorous appreciation of your body. If strong you can throw him from side to side of the bed; this will be his experience of sex inside a tumble dryer. You will clamber on top, arch your back and sink your fingernails into his chest like some ebullient bird of prey. Yet you will growl. A successful bout of coition will finish with your throwing him on top of you with detailed instructions as to rate and depth of penetration.

And It Has To Be Said

Everyone wishes you wouldn't yodel during your sexual crisis. They do not find it attractive no matter what they say.

Aphrodisiacs

You love successful people who have drugs and comfortable cars and who can help you with your career. You also like gypsies, and delivery boys, bikies, and men with pendulous organs that swing slowly as they walk. You like cowboys who can talk. Though you are at first susceptible to meat, you need mental stimulation to do it again.

Deviating

In the early stages of a romance you may coyly enjoy a masterful hand turning you over and driving your face into a pillow – you are hungry for experience, even in preliminary masochism. But soon your natural self-assertion will come forward and bossy instructions in the matter of humiliation will follow. ('Can't you do *anything* without my *telling* you?') You also need many partners in your life, and you will raid their sexual vocabulary, leaving them nothing to say for a very long time after you.

What Aries Knows

People treat you much better if you have shouted at them.

How To Make Aries Like You

You can't. They either like you or they don't. And even if they do like you you shouldn't ever contradict them. Or stand too close to them when they've been drinking. Unless they're *very* drunk indeed, then maybe they won't try to punch you.

Arien Check-List

Talent for freestyle rugby.

Can suffer from giganticism, where feet and hands grow too large.

No member of the Royal Family.

How Aries Suits The Late Twentieth Century

You didn't enjoy the liberal consensus much, and you were depressed prior to that (you hate rationing and service discipline). You will probably enjoy the next few years rather more than any time since the 1920s. You may make a lot of money (mad, thrusting entrepreneurs are getting a good press) and your brand of freelance fascism is almost respectable. Taxes are coming down, incentives are going up, and Mrs Thatcher will see the century out. But be careful – she may be forced onwards through the Zodiac by pressure within her party, so make the most of it now.

Those Born Under Aries

Rolf Harris, Michael Parkinson, Marshall of the RAF Sir Arthur 'Bomber' Harris, Werner von Braun, Sir Alec Guinness, Bette Davis, Cecily Courtneidge, Sir John Gielgud, Neil Kinnock, Norman Tebbit, Tony Benn, David Steele, Ian Paisley, Papa Doc Duvalier, Mrs Bandaranaike, Malcolm Muggeridge, Mary

Pickford, Omar Shariff, Peter Ustinov, Jeffrey Archer, David Frost, Renee Descartes, Hugh Hefner, Eric von Daniken, Bishop Abel Muzorewa, Algy Cluff, Baudelaire, Andrew and Julian Lloyd Webber, Michael York, Spike Milligan, Tennessee Williams, Dirk Bogarde, Anita Bryant, Eric Clapton, Hayley Mills, Rachmaninov, Isambard Brunel, Vivien Nicholson, Eric Idle, Stephen Sondheim, Chapman Pincher, Sarah Vaughan, Margaret Price, Loretta Lynn, Dusty Springfield, Dame Bridget D'Oyly Carte, David Cassidy, Simone Signoret, the San Francisco Earthquake, Lindsay Anderson, Francis Ford Coppola, James Garner, Ian Richardson, Patrick Garland, Mary Moore, Tom Lehrer, Paul Robeson, Joseph Pulitzer, Edward Fox, Baroness Magham, Marty Wilde, Lucrezia Borgia, Kruschev, Leonardo da Vinci, Leslie Thomas, Jimmy Edwards, Tommy Trinder, ex-Queen Alexandra of Yugoslavia, Humphrey Burton, Robert Fox, Paul Glaser, David Lean, Lord Quinton, A. J. P. Taylor, Bartok, Boulez, Carol Carr, Leonard Nimoy, Diana Ross, Chico Marx, St Theresa of Avila, Pearl Bailey, Debbie Reynolds, Carol White, Paul Gambaccini, John Virgo, Lord Jellicoe, Jane Asher, Gregory Peck, Steve McQueen, Clyde Barrow, Elton John, Claudia Cardinale, Flora Robson, Richard Stilgoe, Gloria Swanson, Jack Jones, Van Gogh, Warren Beatty, John Fowles, Richard Chamberlain, Edgar Wallace, Casanova, Doris Day, Marlon Brando, Mary Hemingway, Spencer Tracy, Butch Cassidy, Andre Previn, Billy Holliday, Mary Pickford, Valerie Singleton, Jeremy Beadle, Alan Ayckbourn, F. W. Woolworth, Joe Davis, Charlie Chaplin, Kingsley Amis, Elizabeth Jane Howard, Henry Kelly, Clare Francis, Dudley Moore, Jayne Mansfield, and the hideous Gloria Hunniford.

TAURUS

(21 April – 21 May)

Smart people tell us how middle-class the Queen and her values are, so it is appropriate for Her Majesty to have been born on the first day of the intensely bourgeois sign of Taurus. She shares the sign with Denis Thatcher.

The Karma Involved

The Queen's soul (and Denis Thatcher's) have chosen this incarnation in Taurus to demonstrate to themselves that there is no security in this world of change, to experience the hollowness of material ambition. Bound by possessions to the Wheel of Life, Taurean souls struggle to release themselves from the pain-filled illusions of permanence, stability and property. It appears Her Majesty still has some work to do here. King Karl Gustav of Sweden and ex-Queen Juliana of the Netherlands have done better. The Emperor Hirohito of Japan has done so well he will be graduating into Gemini. Denis Thatcher will be posted back to Aries.

The Social Handicaps

Taurus is the sign of deferred gratification, of tax plans and savings schemes, of food processors and three-piece suites, of La-Zee-Boy reclining armchairs and Atomic coffee makers. Taureans are solid, acquisitive, reliable burghers. They Pay As They Earn. Sir Arthur Sullivan was Taurean, Arthur Marshall still is, but David Jacobs lost his Taurean status when he lost his job at *Any Questions*. Redundancy is the one thing Taureans fear more than death. Taureans work steadily and hard during the day, then watch television until nine, with half a dream of mortgages. Taureans never shared toys as children. Taureans still curl an arm round their homework. Taureans hurry into a submissive posture in the presence of authority (ref Sir Hew '*Royal Heritage*' Wheldon), even when in authority themselves.

Your Taurean Interests

Your Taurean interests include the guttering and the double glazing. Both Karl Marx and Lenin mixed these with an interest in economics (money is another Taurean concern). Your curiosity about the world outside Rose Cottage extends to wondering how much money it has. Your bank manager is fond of you. You reply to his letters. But you're never sufficiently overdrawn to inspire real affection. However you may end up becoming bank managers yourselves (both Guy de and Jacob Rothschild are significant Taureans), though if you achieve any real success you will have something to do with the land (it's the subsidies) – Taurean failures end up as real-estate agents.

The largest part of your emotional commitments are invested in your home. Here is the central heating, here is the budget account for new acquisitions. Where is the wife? She is somewhere too. Here are the *chisels*.

What Your Aura Says

There is something awful about Taureans. Possibly it's the car coats you wear for your Sunday afternoon drives around the Common. You can often be union officials, horse trainers, quite successful welterweights. In the Taurean soul it's always Sunday afternoon four hours before the pubs open. There is a repressed, deeply depressing sense of rationing about you: the sixties made no impression on you, and you're rather proud of it, glad to stay identified with Taureans Lonnie Donegan and Derek Guyler. There is a suffocating suburban solidity about you – Terry Scott and Thelwell (first name, significantly Taurean, *Norman*) – your houses are pleasant semis with a banked drive which you concreted yourself. You live in avenues with rowan trees, you tune in to fellow Taurean Roy Hudd's weekly comedy news programme *Huddlines*, and you actually laugh. You also laughed whole-heartedly at the other Taurean comedian Tony Hancock. Like calls to like, sun sign vibrates to sun sign. You can look Eric Sykes in the face without loss of spirits.

Your acquisitive instinct applies itself to everything. Like the Arien you collect information, but unlike the Arien you can process it into experience. Your deep purpose is to learn the hollowness of material ambition, but if Her Majesty is failing in this mature ambition, what chance has Denis Thatcher?

You have a loud, unmusical voice and often a rather bovine face. (Ella Fitzgerald is a partial exception to this). There is a monotonous rhythm to your intellectual processes, and everyone knows what you're going to say well before you've said it.

So ponderously confident are you that you have something useful to offer that it is as well your practical sense has given you an instinct for self-sufficiency. A disproportionate number of Taureans are born into the aristocracy (both Dukes Wellington and Ellington) or they can drift up through higher financial management to become chairman of building societies or the BBC. Much of the stultification of British industry can be ascribed to the conservative sloth and profound self-interest of this Taurean influence. The monotonous certainty which you bring to your views and expression mean that you do well in politics, and indeed the middle management of both parties – all the politicians you have never heard of: Robert Key, Archy Kirkwood, John Maples, Ian Twinn, Lord Diamond, Fred Warner, Eddie Loyden, Michael McGuire – are born under the sign of Taurus. They may not be very clever, but then 'We don't set much store on *cleverness* at Albion House'. They are reliable, their strongest asset is their appetite for party discipline, they have *bottom*, they know their mind. If only they had the slightest flair they might be better known off the two square feet of their back benches.

As a Taurean you lack that telegenic gloss that is attractive to the 1980s. *Poor old* Henry Cooper is a Taurean. However – a flight of fancy – you can be socially ambitious and at your small, infrequent, but rather well-catered parties, we may be sure of one or two celebrities – the borough surveyor perhaps, or a qualified architect.

Patient, Browsing Herbivores

Yours is the sign of the silent majority, a negative, stoical, anal sign, full of fortitude. You can carry on for years, taking your greatest pleasure in paying large insurance premiums, getting wearier and wearier, worrying about the reckless spending of the modern world. You may die before expressing yourselves, and this is just as well, because when your rage breaks, everything is laid to waste. And it isn't just faces exploding under the great beef of your hand, but a greater social hostility that infects those around you, and through them, the state itself. There is a darkness in the heart of the bull.

Do you doubt your real worth? Why else do you accumulate so steadily? The more you have the less you are. The artificial order and stability you impose on your surroundings (many of those MPs are fierce for law and order) may be to protect yourself from the disorder you fear in your own personality, the Taurean's deep fear of spontaneity. It is a dark pit down there, and who knows what comes out of it when it is stirred. And many things do stir you.

There comes a time when there is just one too many feminists for you, one too many Leninists, one too many clever men, fancy men, pansies, anarchists, radicals, madmen, Jonathan Millers being thrust into our faces in our living rooms ('I look on it as though they've been invited into my home – and they behave in a way no guest should'). In times of prosperity you will soldier on in your deeply unfashionable serge suit and company tie. No amount of social unrest will shake you – bombing, rioting, striking, starvation in the North, repossession orders will not move you to action. But when inflation devalues your currency, fear works on you. The core of your acquisitive being is stirred and the Silent Majority opens its pit. A decent man can only take so many deviants, degenerates, punks, drunks, Jews and gypsies. Only so many meddlers, progressives, paedophiles, drug peddlers, academics, aerobics teachers, speculators, developers, foreigners, French films. Only so much free credit, mass education, laxity, laxatives, liberal reformers, and craven magistrates. The vast class of Taurus can only be pushed so far. But when inflation devalues your savings, your investments, your portfolios they push you towards the edge, and you will retaliate.

Thus Taurus offers a much more complete description of the Nazi personality than the impetuous and spontaneous Aries. The petty bourgeois, anal-retentive, authority-respecting, grasping, stubborn, self-disciplined, big bodied counter-clerks with their well-brought-up, soundly disciplined, clean-limbed little boys and girls with their little pigtails and clean hands, are the fascist's natural power base. There is a methodical, deliberate, purposeful link between disorder in the money markets and the gassing of six million Jews. 'Nothing *like* six million,' Taureans may still say, 'it's been proven that the real figure was actually barely *three* million.' The most striking thing about the extermination was the quality of steady bureaucratic routine that characterized it – a very Taurean trait.

Interestingly, the *Daily Mail* was first published under Taurus in 1896. And Adolf Hitler was born under Taurus just a few years before.

What Taurus Knows

That it will be the dickens of a job getting those demons let out in the sixties back into the bottle.

That there is no such thing as a free lunch.

That tomorrow is another day, and that the one after that is another one too.

That it's not really worth people working as they can make more money on the dole, and that this is clearly the real cause of structural unemployment.

That an Englishman's home is his castle.

That the police do a magnificent job under impossible conditions.

That women are race of alien beings deposited on the earth by a malevolent judiciary in another star system.

Few Friends But Good Ones

When asked how you are you may well say, 'In rude health, my masters!' (David Attenborough rarely says anything else.) If for no other reason, you find it difficult to make new friends. However you are more reliable than the more gregarious signs, your friendship is more secure, and by natural fiscal law your terms are more severe.

You are put to a variety of uses by the friends who seek you out: women use you for reassurance (they sense there is something inside you, and they like this until they find out what it is); men use you as a companion for watching television, or to check out the motors of cars they want to buy. You are a useful reference for all sorts of things: you are expert in pricing spark plugs; you know whether they need a 100 watt or 60 watt bulb in the bathroom, you know how many miles to the gallon all major brands do in town and highway driving, and you know the quickest way from Essex to Leatherhead. You will reluctantly lend your electric saw, your electric drill, but never your chisels ('They're like fountain pens, a foreign hand will damage the nib').

Great Strength of Character

You have no nerves, and no sense of humour, but how you laugh when you see a fat woman going over. When she hits the ground and her foundation garments go, and her big floppy body bursts into the room from her underwear you go weak with laughter, you actually do hold your ribs, you really do slap your thigh.

However, you never complain. Unfortunately that's how women get to know men, so you Taureans remain a mystery for longer than any other sign (except Geminis who can never be adequately explained, even with professional help).

Things Taureans Say

'Let's get our feet back on the ground.'

'Let's get our heads out of cloud cuckoo land.'

'All right, all right, settle down, joke over.'

(If Fred Astaire) 'I'm the luckiest hoofer and the luckiest guy in the whole world.'

In Business

You lack a talent for casual cruelty and this can hold you back in your career. It is one of many things that hold you back. A general satisfaction with your position in the firm, and the avenue you live in don't help you on to greater things. You are drawn to the countryside – the idiocy of rural life suits you, and unless you were born with an inheritance, or unless you marry into it, your profit from the land will be modest. However, you are never in a hurry to make a decision, you always get a good price for anything you have to sell, and you generally make an excellent peasant. You are a nightmare for salesmen. You never sign anything for as long as you can possibly leave it. You prefer to wait until the goods have been sold to someone else, before you commit yourself to buying.

Money comes to you – you are shrewd, patient, and you will contentedly wait forever for the chance of a lifetime to come along. But when it does, as it inevitably will (*vide* the British Telecom issue) you will fail to realize every penny of cash you can, content to apply for a couple of hundred shares 'as a flutter'. You make good book-keepers, but barely adequate accountants as you lack the flair to make a column of positive figures add up to a tax deduction.

Your major virtue is loyalty to your employer, and this is why you are generally paid less than colleagues doing comparable jobs. You assume you will be reimbursed fairly, and everyone else assumes you are retarded. However, you are sure of your rights, and on those occasions when you are unable to generate a sense of grievance you will stubbornly pursue what you believe to be just. This lack of flexibility, in a time when flexibility is prized as a talent, goes down on your record. Even in the sunset industries this is less and less of a good thing. Even in building societies. Your resistance to change, invention, innovation, ('Let's get our feet back on the ground for a moment, shall we?') was useful as long as the current was running too fast, but now that things have slowed, more attack is required. Your tremendous inertia when confronted with something new and obviously attractive is appalling to innovators. You would have found half a dozen objections to demoralize the inventor of word-processing machines. 'If it's such a good idea,' you will say in a tone of worldly resignation, 'someone would have done it already.' It is even more satisfying when you can say, '*Ah* yes, that's a frightfully good idea, *so* frightfully good in fact it's been done already.' You never get used to being called a dunderhead either. Colleagues have to let you demolish any new idea as wishful pie-in-the-sky impractical, idealistic flim-flammery, so that you can reinvent it and represent it as your own. As this process can take two or three years your colleagues place their faith elsewhere.

Luckily for you, promotion is rarely a product of talent or aptitude, and much more a question of staying in the same place for long enough. Your very steadiness allows you to be promoted well beyond the level of your capabilities.

As a manager you can make an efficient, strict, detail-conscious housemaster who carries a battery of different-coloured pentels for issuing policy statements. Obviously you don't know how to deal with the clever boys but then you don't set much store by cleverness. You are a natural employee. Not a pleasant job, but *someone's* got to do it.

How To Make A Mess Of A Taurean In The Boardroom

As they love detailed administration they can be unsettled by broad policy discussion. They are susceptible to intellectual agoraphobia, and wide-ranging discussion will make them visibly anxious.

A change of direction, if precisely timed, can make them burst into tears. Just when they thought they were getting the hang of the debate's terms of reference, shift the grounds to Tokyo, or 1990, or into the next oil crisis. Don't let their look of bewilderment melt your purpose.

Their meticulous attention to priorities suggests they can be driven to a nervous breakdown by conflicting demands of equal weight. Appoint him as a mediator between vital departments. You may have to diversify into hostile product categories to make the conflict sufficiently stark to bring about the nervous breakdown. Often there is no other way of getting rid of the devoted Taurean.

Physically

You have a good heart, but this is no excuse for the melon belly you generally develop (Orson Welles has the classic Taurean build). Your fine musculature can degenerate in early middle age into porkiness – sexual frustration is taken out in the restaurant. You sublimate greed into gourmandizing. Clement Freud is the caution for all Taureans in this regard. On the good side your bowels are regular, but you are prey to wind, and your arse can bark fiercely in the street. You also leave a sour smell on the back of your shirts, your sheets and your pyjamas; this is complemented by the bitter smell of manly breath around your mouth and under your jaw.

Taureans suffer from poor circulation, weak ankles, varicose veins, obesity, lethargy and kidney infections. Apart from this you are generally robust.

Romantically

Venus is the ruler of your sign, so there is something worth attending to in your sexual expression. The syntax may be simple but it is undeniably effective: Nureyev and Valentino were both born under this sign. Women with low self-esteem and limited body image find you immensely reassuring in the early stages. The slow burn of your banked fires gives off a glow to which they are drawn. As you say of wine you bring to a party, 'It may not be very nice but there's an awful lot of it.'

Women also like you because such intelligence as you have does not threaten them. Geminis and Librans can frighten women with their cold perceptions. You are happy to state the reassuringly obvious with such a show of finding it interesting (it isn't actually a show) that girls warm to you with an '*Ahhhhh*!' They think you're a big soppy old softie. Their light, carbonated intelligence offers them a feeling of effortless superiority. This will last well into the relationship, right up to the time they realize they haven't been taken dancing for over a year, you haven't got off the sofa the whole weekend, and you've started farting in bed. '*Oh* yes,' your frisky wife will say, 'you're dependable all right, you're *dependable*, you're so fucking *dependable* you make me *sick*!' 'Who can figure women?' you will wonder.

Taurus Courtship

You tend not to make the running, but stand around waiting for someone to be drawn into orbit by the force of your gravity. You are not gay in your courting mode. You rarely laugh, and when you do it has a sinister quality, like a customs officer laughing. Your wooing is policeman-like: pedestrian but effective. All too soon you will be introducing your thick sensual fingers to the inside of her underwear – your friends will wonder how you do it, what these girls see in you. So do the girls.

You often rely on being a member of the Royal Family to be your most attractive feature.

Actually Doing It

You don't enjoy foreplay but it is expected these days, and you don't want to seem eccentric. In the more obviously pleasurable stages you will wallow in sex, burying your nose in the long trough, truffling for pleasure. Though desire inevitably fails your appetite returns regularly, and this is the best chance you have for sustaining your marriage. Some women (Scorpions, Aquarians, Leos) need sex in the same way they need food – without it they wither. Make sure you marry one such.

You tend to get on top fairly quickly and get busy without frills. If she refuses to turn over you may enter from behind. This will be mistaken for urgent desire in the early days. It may even be desire, but when it decays to appetite she will not be able to tell the difference, precisely when it changed. She will say at some point, later, 'There was a time when he used to wrap me in himself and engulf me with warmth. Now he just squashes me.'

When you get fat together you like to rub your large stomachs against each other's, you find it intimate, erotic, sharing your investments. You tend to blow heavily at climax, and then relax (the squashing comes in here). Alone in the Zodiac you do not resent it when she says 'Hold me,' or 'Tell me a story.' You will indeed hold her, but as you fall asleep immediately a story is out of the question.

You Can't Abide

Women who want you to talk to them during congress.

Hunt saboteurs.

Post-Suez smart farts.

Women who are full of themselves, and who get on top with an overconfident look on their faces.

Taureans Often Say

'You can't change human nature.'

'If money can't buy you happiness at least you can be miserable in comfort.'

'If you knew how ridiculous you looked you'd be *so bloody* embarrassed!'

Women

Taurean women enjoy an annual convention at the Conservative Party Conference. They identify themselves by waving handcuffs at each other and baying for the return of the birch.

They offer to apply it themselves: 'Did me no harm as a girl, wouldn't do me any harm now,' they say, with a determined look under their hats.

You make outstanding bossy old trouts (Barbara Woodhouse, Florence Nightingale, Eva Peron) and have a strong sense of your position in society – often at the top of your circle. Your acute sense of the meticulous leads you to the presidency of the Tenants' Association. You also make diligent monarchs. A surprising proportion of the blood royal incarnates under Taurus – Zara Phillips, Lady Gabriella Windsor, Her Majesty herself, Catherine the Great, Lord Lichfield, Lady Sarah Armstrong-Jones, etc. etc.

Your Girth Expands With Your Responsibilities

You enjoy a splendid vitality, but you can run to plumpness (Nellie Melba, who had several dozen ice-creams named after her, and Fats Waller, who had several dozen children named after him – both classic Taurean builds). Taureans are mainly excited by sex, food and possessions – often getting the former through the latter two. The Magimix is a potent blend of symbols.

You may take out your sexual frustrations in the kitchen, and this doesn't help. You often give up and relax into matronhood around your early thirties. This is the result of your sex life, your marriage, and your appearances at the Tory Convention in Brighton.

The major organs of assault, doctors tell us, are in the upper front body. For Taureans this denotes the bosoms. For men married to Taurean women the major organ of assault is the heart: the hi-fat diet she puts you on (along with the wheedling, 'What's the matter? Didn't you like the dinner? Aren't you hungry? Don't you want to finish up the suet for Mummy?') offers the best odds for a major embolism in your middle-fifties.

Your Home

You like to live in the deep suburbs, out beyond the ring road. If you stand in the spare bedroom and look out over beyond the housing estates you can see wheat fields. A semi is best as it gives you contact with the outside world (something that doesn't come naturally to you). You must have a long strip of garden backing on to playing fields, with mature fruit trees, flower beds, and in January a carpet of snowdrops, the first flowers of the year, under the crooked apple trees. You will turn the fish pond into a sandpit until your babies have learned to swim. The little things will waddle up to the shed and hide there, and shriek when you find them. On summer evenings you will have reclining deck chairs out on the flagging, and have two drinks, as the children chase balls on their little brown legs, before their baths, and bed. To preserve this against the world you would agree to anything, even the gassing of unattractive minorities. You draw a very hard line, harder than your male counterpart. You protect your family at all costs, from anything, absolutely anything (you do not include yourself in this anything).

Recreations

Mulching compost.

Baking for *half* the price of shop-bought.

Cancelling her magazine after 20 years' subscription following an entirely unwarranted journalistic attack.

Intelligence

Selina Scott, named by a Daily Mirror poll as one of the five most intelligent women in Britain is Taurean. However Joanna Lumley and Liberace are Taurean too, so the evidence must be split. When you go the wrong way you turn into Shirley McClaine and talk to spacemen.

You have a sharp eye for what suits you best, and you can build your self-interest into a general theory of social and moral relations. The Royal Family are attractive examples of this tendency. However, such mental talents as you have can be obscured by the neurotic insecurity that binds you to your monotonous habits. You will go on the same holiday, to the same place, year after year, even though you didn't like it the first time you went, or indeed on any subsequent year. 'Oh well, better the devil you know,' you say when you arrive, and 'I shall be glad to get home,' when you leave. Lack of pleasure is a small price to pay for security, and anyway you are now accustomed to not enjoying your holidays – pleasure would make you deeply anxious.

Career

Your slow, painstaking approach makes you unsuitable for most interesting jobs but you do make a competent public servant, especially in departments where delay has achieved traditional status. You also make a dreadful waitress, but can administer a tight budget with strength and discipline, and no imagination.

You are fair prey for fringe entrepreneurs who need part-time workers to labour at sweatshop rates – a combination of your low self-esteem, and your marketplace philosophy of labour supply. In this you are incredibly stubborn and will turn down pay awards to prove your point.

However, you are better suited to the middle eighties than more sensitive, intelligent, idealistic, questioning signs – this is not an age of doubt, it is an age of certainty. An age of certainty and of anger. Everyone knows best, and if you don't you will be elbowed aside by those who do. You lack the anger but the certainty is yours – you are at least on-side, you are in the newly respectable majority of mutes.

As The Centre Of The Household

As you were a responsible little thing (and affectionate too, you remember) you can't understand why your children resent you so much. You do not see how overbearing you can be, and how penetrating. Your fingers find their way into all their secret places, leaving them no privacy. You can also compete with your daughters – you will win at first, but it is later than you think, and they're already much slimmer than you.

In regard to your husband, you can be the ideal wife for either a clever adulterer (you will never give him a divorce – the last thing he actually wants), but you would prefer a reliable proto-Nazi much like yourself. You will endure pain and poverty rather than leave your husband. You feel immensely superior to men, especially a lightweight, and will bear down on him over the years using your capacity for affection, and the provision of regular meals to keep him close to you. 'Habit', Sartre said, 'is the ballast that chains a dog to his vomit,' and this is just as well.

You are even-tempered, and respond well to regular servicing. You are also inexpensive to run – very few drugs, a little red wine, great tuns of pâté are all you need. A handful of flowers will reduce you to a state of pathetic gratitude.

Your unswerving devotion to the home will increasingly irritate your husband through the first seven years. 'Why don't you *do* something instead of just *sitting* there *sewing*?' he will say. The expression of bewildered pain spreading across your facescape will make him feel like a dog.

You will rise to the intellectual challenge of running a home and enjoy the intellectual exercise of reconciling your stubs with your statements. You operate best on a tight budget.

Sexually

You like big wet-liver kisses. You salivate and over-lubricate. Kissing a Taurean woman is like being hit in the face with a wet teabag.

Owing to your difficulties with your mad body as a child (big hands, uncoordinated legs, beefy face) you can still suffer from a low body image and you may be subject to limited self esteem as a result. Perhaps it is this that makes you so anxious for security, so cautious about revealing yourself. However, as you learn to trust a man more and more you will strip more and more layers to reveal your self in its primal molten state. Ariel Automatic is the only detergent that works on your bed linen.

Early experiences will have found you as the patient in any game of Doctors on the block. 'Just let me take your temperature my dear, get out the old pork thermometer shall we? – Perhaps we'd better get a second opinion from Doctor Leroy, what's your prognosis? Bleep Doctor Winston will you – he specializes in Ear, Nose and Throat, it's lucky we're in a group practice, my dear.'

Your major sexual characteristic is, notwithstanding, great enthusiasm for sex. You project a tremendous sense of erotic sensuality but you only get naked with a *great deal* of forethought. When you do get going however you are demanding. You have a libido as big as a liver gone bad. When your passion is released it flashes over your partner and sticks to him like napalm. He feels flash-fried. He feels his willy has been plugged into the National Grid – a certain sort of man may enjoy this.

Taurean women require complete attention in the matter of sex: it doesn't seem much to ask, but men have wandering minds and may need to take drugs to command their presence in the business. The apparently endless interval between your ignition and lift-off will exhaust many men. And they gasp, and their lungs go, and their hair sticks to their foreheads and they slide around on top of you in the slick of sex. You have a great time. And the things they say about you in the locker room aren't really justified, because at least you don't lie there like a beached fish. At least you clutch and grip and beg for more (even though there isn't any more to give).

There will grow a look in your eye which will put men off towards the end of your sexual life (about age 37). You will realise how little sex you've actually had, and how little else there actually is in life. A sudden give in the stomach will frighten you and you'll realize how cautious you were as a 25-year-old, how pleased you were with your high moral tone. The older you get, the stronger your confidence, and the more sexually demanding you will become. This will be in precise proportion to your weight gain. The more demanding you become the higher the price will be driven, and the less you will be given – this is the economic law you admire so much at the Conservative Party Conference. When roused you will be insatiable. As a 40-year-old fatty you will remain so – you lack the emotional equipment to wheel in specialists and marathon men.

Your Fantasy

That Bruce Springsteen will fall in love with you, marry you, give up rock and roll and get a job managing an import/export company.

Advice To Men

When she finally does give herself she gives herself completely. This can dismay men, particularly those who don't want her. For this reason she has learnt caution, and the rate of exchange for her emotional currency. If you are sharply rebuffed by a Taurean do not think she is necessarily uninterested in you. You may simply be moving too quickly. She may well be receptive to a manly thrust into her territory. But be warned that Taurus is the sign of ownership: the slow trade will be her way of building the best bargain she can. The concept of recreational sex is alien to her, as is recreational shopping. 'You get nothing for nothing in this life,' she says *and she's right!*

The Taurean woman desires to submit to her man, but do not let this confuse you. Her submission does not mean you are winning. The dominant is bound to the submissive. The sadist needs the masochist more than vice versa. She submits only to improve her bargaining base.

Bring presents. Lavish compliments upon her. She will believe anything, no matter how far fetched. Fill her with five-star food. Don't flirt with her by telling her you want to put your head up her dress. She wants to be persuaded you are a serious person. She doesn't find low talk attractive or amusing, just childish. Show your credit cards. Bring her roses. Let her sit in the back of your Bentley and, without warning, push your head up her dress – don't ask if you may (she'll always say no, but she would regret it when she was 37).

Taurean Secret

She needs respect more than love.

She Knows

Waste not, want not.

Men are only after one thing.

The way to a man's heart is through his stomach.

Real men don't eat quiche (she doesn't know what real men do eat – *shit*, every day of their lives).

Taurean Members

Arthur English, H.M. the Queen, Studs Turkel, Adolf Hitler, Denis Thatcher, King Karl Gustav of Sweden, ex-Queen Juliana of the Netherlands, the Emperor Hirohito of Japan, Sir Arthur Sullivan, Arthur Marshall, David Jacobs, Sir Hew Wheldon, Karl Marx, Lenin, Guy de Rothschild, Jacob Rothschild, Lonnie Donegan, Derek Guyler, Terry Scott, Norman Thelwell, Roy Hudd, Tony Hancock, Eric Sykes, Ella Fitzgerald, Duke

Ellington, the Duke of Wellington, Henry Cooper, Lord Beeching, Sir Thomas Beecham, Sir Malcolm Sargent, William Randolph Hearst, Sandra Dee, The Earl of Lichfield, Buster Mottram, Al Pacino, William Roache, Carol Burnett, Charlie Chester, Bernard Malamud, Morris West, Anouk Aimee, John Mortimer, Lord Harlech, Norman Parkinson, Leo Abse, Yehudi and Hepzibah Menuhin, Kathleen Ferrier, Shirley McLaine, Barbra Streisand, Clement Freud, Sigmund Freud, Anthony Trollope, Walter de la Mare, Lady Hamilton, Anita Loos, C. Day Lewis, Glenn Cambell, George Cole, Billy Cotton, J. P. Donleavy, Earl of Drogheda, Bernadette McAliskey, Lee Majors, Roy Orbison, Lady Gabby Windsor, Turner, Jack Klugman, Bing Crosby, Dr Benjamin Spock, Joanna Lumley, David Coleman, Henry Cooper, Mrs Golda Meir, Englebert Humperdink, Terry Scott, Audrey Hepburn, El Cordobes, Valentino, Orson Welles, Mike Brearly, Kenneth Kaunda, Jack Nicholson, Zubin Mehta, Jeremy Thorpe, Jill Clayburg, David Attenborough, Barbara Woodhouse, Joan Sims, Fred Astaire, Eric Morecombe, Richard Avedon, Liberace, Bernard Braden, Rod McKuen, Margot Fonteyn, Perry Como, Victoria Wood, Nellie Melba, Nancy Astor, James Stewart, Henri Rousseau, Desmond Wilcox, Fats Waller, Raymond Burr, Malcolm Fraser, Dickie Davies, Lord Peart, Lady Sarah Armstrong-Jones, Glenn Ford, Joseph Heller, Julian Mitchell, Rear Admiral Sir John Woodward, Bianca Jagger, Clive Jenkins, Satyajit Ray, Isla St Clair, Terry Duffy, Peter Oosterhuis, John Sachs, John Speke, Dr Hugh Jolly, Michael Palin, Steward Granger, Robin Hanbury-Tenison, Richard O'Sullivan, Peter Benchley, Jack Charlton, Alan Bennett, Candice Bergen, Glenda Jackson, Billy Joel, Colonel Blood, Richard Adams, Monica Dickens, Donovan, Maureen Lipman, Sugar Ray Robinson and Leonard, Irving Berlin, Dr Rhodes Boyson, Eric Burdon, Phil Silvers, Burt Bacharach, Leslie Charteris, Ian Dury, Wilfred Hyde-White, Lord Kaldor, Rt Rev Hugh Montefiore, Miriam Stoppard, Edward Lear, Jane Glover, Zoe Wanamaker, Stevie Wonder, Chay Blyth, Sian Phillips, Constance Cummings, Ted Dexter, Zara Phillips, Anthony and Peter Shafter, Ralph Steadman, Olga Korbut, Frank Capra, Lord Hartwell, Norman

St John Stevas, Rick Wakeman, Toyah Willcox, Charles Wintour, Bertrand Russell, Mark Boxer, Calman, Edward de Bono, James Fox, Pete Townshend, Sandy Wilson, Cher, John Stuart Mill, Dandy Nichols, Leo Sayer, and Alexander Pope.

GEMINI

(22 May – 21 June)

When they discover you are a Gemini no one ever quite trusts you again. As though you had a bankruptcy in your background, or a first wife or payslips from *Private Eye*, or a history of alcoholism. No matter how solid you appear there will always be suspected a radical defect in the Gemini psyche. This is unsurprising in George Best and Jean-Paul Sartre, but it is disturbing to learn that the Duke of Edinburgh is a Gemini.

The First Impact

You are intensely friendly and communicative. Strangers assume you're on coke. You worry everyone within striking distance. Your moods change in astounding dislocations, your conversation flickers at stroboscopic speed. This is true of all Geminis except Bjorn Borg who is the opposite – a typically Gemini trait.

You are the first sign of the zodiac to be aware of the outside world – the impact was shattering. Your personality has been splashed into a dozen fractured identities, most of which you are barely aware of. There is something deeply diabolical about this. God is Himself and nothing else, eternal, unchanging. Like Lord Beaverbrook. It is the Devil who assumes many shapes, often for discreditable purposes. Also like Lord Beaverbrook – this is the duality of the Gemini soul. However, tradition tells us that you have a deeply spiritual nature, and you read magazines from the back.

The Karma

You have checked into this sign to learn that the mind is the great organ of *maya*, of deception and illusion, of passing through one mental mood to another as though through dreams. The creator of proto-existentialism, the Marquis de Sade, was one of the first Geminis. Your task is to learn that the physical world exists, and then to learn that it is not real. That the material universe is but a hologram projected on to four-dimensional space-time by an unknowable, pre-Platonic projectionist. You must achieve a Zen state of unaware awareness to realize this.

This isn't always as easy as it sounds.

You're So Contemporary

You are very quick. You chatter like a pair of castanets. You get rowdy in print. You belong to the Communication Class, the KGB of capitalism. All Fleet Street editors are Geminis – Peter Preston of the *Guardian*, Bill Deedes of the *Daily Telegraph*, Anthony Shrimsley, late of the *Daily Mail*, Sir David English, currently of the *Daily Mail*, J.W.M. Thompson of the *Sunday Telegraph*, and Robert Maxwell, who does everything but edit the *Mirror*. Lord Beaverbrook was a Gemini. James Cameron was a Gemini.

Geminis can be artistic but your major creativity goes into filling out your expenses, and these often read like a comic novel. You are good at scoffing drugs and swatting volleys at the opposition's feet. You generate crippling phone bills. You know less than it seems but you enjoy flashes of concentration. You do seven things at once: six lines of coke and a course of cello lessons. You are versatile, often to the point of schizophrenia. You make a dazzling fly-half (William Pitt the Younger was a fly-half) and can change direction through 180 degrees without stopping. This is useful, but you resemble a sail without a ship – a kite, a windsurfer, a hang glider. This is known on Fleet Street as being a real pro. You travel so fast you have to travel alone and you can be lonely because of it.

Your loneliness is accentuated by the fact that you are weird. Those close to you assume you are simply incoherent, or coked up, or greedy for money, but sooner or later they will find out that you are weird. However you generally do not have serious enemies, unless you marry them.

The Duality Of The Twins

The perfect expression of the astrological double act is the Gemini event of 1953 – Hilary and Tensing, descending Everest, already quarrelling about who pulled whom up on to the summit.

The Random Gemini

Lord Grenfell is a Gemini, the Duke of Bedford is a Gemini, Barry Manilow and Ken Livingstone are Geminis. As a reaction to your inner confusion you may groom yourself to a picture of cautious, conservative respectability. Often you carry it off for years. But one drink too many and you'll suddenly lose it and look peculiar, and assume a lupine grin, and write out a will and sign it Alex. 'Who's *Alex** Rrrrrick?' your wife will ask, but you will only smile, wolfily.

On the other hand, you can just give in to your astrology which offers the crazed eclecticism of Bob Dylan – it's a reasonable living if you can take the touring and the crew sluts.

However you explain yourself you are too clever to give

* Alex was a droog.

anything away. You learned language to disguise your thoughts.

Gadget Consciousness

You believe that he who dies with the most toys . . . wins. You buy home computers, and hover mowers, and key rings with a torch in them to illuminate the keyhole. You invented the guillotine, (Joseph Guillotin), the Cuban revolution (Che Guevara), the tipping theatre seat (Steele MacKaye) and the dustbuster (it doesn't work).

Socially

Yap yap yap yap. Yap yap yap yap yap yap yap yap. *Yap* yap yap yap yap yap yap *yap yap yap*.

Your small talk is brilliant, but you lack warmth, sincerity, heart. You are skilled at making contact without content, establishing relations without revelations – a technique pioneered by Gemini Queen Victoria. At your best you have the ability to articulate a relationship into its narrative verses rather than throwing everything into one dense lyric where everything happens at once. Though often you just bang on the wine gums, too impatient to do anything other than tell your partner absolutely everything you know about yourself. This creates a false impression of shared confidences, and your partner may start telling you about themselves. The last thing you want.

You appear to stupid people to be incoherent. But you know what they're going to say before they start, especially if it's critical (you are a dextrous paranoid).

Health

Though you need pressure and stress to keep you going, personal problems can turn you into a nervous person – your lack of commitment to your body can be damaging, leading to a sense of dissociation. Weak points include your lungs and arms, and you should get a lot of sleep (you never have enough). The lack of personal care (your eating habits are negligible) can hit women harder than men – both physically and socially. You can suffer from anorexia nervosa and/or bulima, or you can suffer from obesity. Some Geminis are fat, others are very fat, yet others have to be stripped naked and greased with butter to force them through a doorway. Only one Gemini is as fat as Robert Morley though.

When your cerebral wiring overloads and blows you do well in certain hospitals. You make excellent volunteers for hi-voltage courses of electric therapy. You feel at home plugged into the national grid. You feel you're looking into the body of God. You're not.

Career

Brilliantly persuasive, you are less brilliant than you appear to be. But then your brilliant talent is precisely to appear to be more brilliant than you actually are. So your hi-energy career starts very promisingly, at Fotomat, or Pizza Hut, and rapidly you achieve executive status: you are goal-oriented; greedy for appreciation, and often this can take the form of money-hunger. You know in your water, though, that you prefer making it to spending it.

You are what the advertising industry calls pro-active. You make incredibly untrustworthy account executives, incredibly unreliable commissioning editors, incredibly random critics (is it a deeply flawed masterpiece or an incoherent rant? A joyous explosion of contemporary emotion, or a self-indulgent embarrassment? A hilarious riot that left you weak with laughter, or a puerile attempt merely to shock? You adopt a statistical approach to the distribution of these phrases – is Milton Schulman a Gemini? He is not listed in *Who's Who*, so nobody knows). You are talented sycophants, but disguise this with cleverly placed misanthropy.

So versatile are you that you can appear to have a sense of humour (Nigel Graffiti Rees is a Gemini), but often you give yourself away by telling Englishmen, Irishmen jokes and leaving humorous messages on your answering machine. You are so unattached to life that you cannot tell what is funny, and you rely on major cues to flag you in. Geminis Bob Hope and Monkhouse aren't funny, but then they have comic timing to disguise the fact. You find release in practical jokes and enjoy nothing more than making a seventy-two hour phone connection to Dial-A-Disc in Los Angeles on someone else's telephone.

You can't bear to be in debt. This doesn't mean you won't borrow money, but it does mean one personality will be paying bank rate to one of your other personalities.

Mouth Do Yo' Stuff

You make bad hacks, good hucksters, active agents, ambitious bargainers, glittering public relations people. You appeal to rich, influential people, and you ache for glamour, city lights, micro-chips, dinner jackets. The Venerable Bede is a typical exception to this Gemini rule but Beau Brummel and John F. Kennedy are not. Geminis find no real satisfaction in the sunset industries with their shrinking villages and long service pensions. You need room to manoeuvre and your footwork is outstanding, but for dancing, not travelling. Even caught with your hands up to the *elbow* in the till you are not at a loss for something to say. But your fast mouth is a two-edged sword, and may lead you into trouble, matrimony, money, prison. You enjoy major career crises (getting fired), often precipitated by discharges from your post-adolescent menopause. The truth is that you find no lasting satisfaction in anything, so embrace a serial career.

What To Do

Mercury, your ruling planet, is the patron saint of editors, orators, switchboard operators, gossips, go-betweens, grapevine artists. You make creative accountants, bad writers, inspirational teachers. You were largely responsible for the sixties.

You motor about and make short, jabbing visits, and this suits you for a whole range of selling jobs, journalism, diabolism. As a middleman you are best, squeezed between commercial imperatives – this ensures some basic predictability in your activities – and it might also develop your potential for two-facedness. This can be one of your major career-tools. You make the best impersonators, but you can also use the flashes of intuition from your multiple personalities to make a reasonable living in the profession of bad acting (something in which Britain leads the world) – at one end Lord Olivier, at the other Simon Callow. Peter Cushing, Vincent Price and Christopher Lee litter the middle ground.

Too-Talented Deceivers

Be careful not to let your excuses become too wild. You are liable to be as surprised as the next man to hear yourself saying, 'I'm sorry, I can't, I'll be in Tokyo, I've got cancer, I was involved in an axe attack in the New King's Road, I'm having my head cut off.'

Your astrology may drive you to fake your credentials. This is quite normal. In job interviews as in war, you reason, the first casualty is Truth. No one will ever ask to see your degree documents. Especially if you have faked a very good degree. The speed of your speech will encourage others to subscribe to your enormous intelligence.

Intellectual challenges enliven you. You do well in, and often win, spelling bees. You have relevant information about almost everything, but very little of it. You win Trivial Pursuits. You know everything you'll never need to know.

Your success and restlessness expose the emptiness of doing well. Money interests you until you have more than enough; fame does the same until you're recognised in the street. You know something real is out there, but you can't make contact with it. This is the tragedy of Geminis. They know they will never get it right. The real world is, however, not out there but in there. The real stuff comes up from deep down – a place Geminis fear doesn't exist.

In Love

You are inclined to make people fall in love with you to see what it's like. It is important for other signs not to sob at you as you will only be interested until their faces go blotchy. At this point you'll go out to dinner. You can't bear to be bored, clung to, grovelled before.

You have a critical tongue, a sharp tongue, you attract and repel simultaneously. This is by design, as your quicksilver sexuality is not satisfied with simplicity. You flirt constantly; even during the most committed acts it is your talent to tease. It is your highest accomplishment – you can be a formal poet seduced by music and rhythms: sounds but no sense. This annoys women. You never give all your heart but can appear to, cleverly over-promising, creating confidence without actually entering into contract. This is useful as you are bored by living with the same person for too long. You need someone who can remodel their personality biennially to hold your interest. Such people are rare, and when you find one it'll probably turn out to be another Gemini.

You are constitutionally dishonest, constitutionally promiscuous, and constitutionally driven to be married more than once. You may suffer from what psychiatrists term 'The Peter Pan Syndrome' indicating a reluctance to grow up, adopt adult responsibilities like talking to your wife at a party and giving up social rugby.

You have very little sense of the flesh, and whether there is any mystery or magic to be conjured from it. You do not understand about pain, and how cruelty hurts. In the imagination, in the shadowplay, bruises are few, and they do not cause pain to you, or ripen. You can be cruel, especially if your partners are slow, pedestrian, careful, susceptible to bewilderment. You will try out your rage on them to see how they perform. You will sulk and slash at the hedgerows with your ash-plant. You will look into a moody sky and write *Byron Is Dead* in the chalk. Or perhaps you will just send out for pizzas. Your elusive quality makes this difficult to tell.

In terms of recreational romance you belong in New York where intimacy on impact – sincere, but short – is a recognized social medium.

Will He Be Faithful?

Yes. He will. He will go to bed with *many* other women, indeed, virtually *every* other woman, but he will remain faithful to you. Once you make contact with the deep spiritual self he tells of, he will be profoundly faithful to you. Though this won't stop him inseminating anything that moves under its own steam. Each of his multiple personalities needs satisfaction, and this will bruise anyone close to you (partners will find difficulty walking in the morning).

Sexually

The shock of sex is great for the Mental – Air – Mutable signs. Big, blind sex organs frighten you. Perhaps this is why you cannot show love, only talk about it. However you make talented sluts, slags and scrubbers (or the male equivalent, good men about town).

Your sexual intercourse may be unsatisfactory – too much like small talk, not enough of the big sonorous paragraphs nor the long, coherent, polemical bursts; nor a sustained rhyme scheme. There is poetry in it though, and you have a big vocabulary. You also have a fund of new and amusing things to say, sexually; clichés don't interest you as they do Taureans. You are capable of surprise and spontaneous response. If a woman expresses her delight at your metropolitan expertise in bed you will not say 'I agree with the Good Doctor that a man who is tired of London is tired of *life*.' However you will be critic as well as creative artist, and you will never really enjoy the mindless potential of extra-cranial sex. As a pure Gemini you will flicker over a body, making use of your bilingual abilities. She will like you for it.

Actually Doing It

There is an Australasian saying: 'Gemini women generally fake orgasms, but alone in the Zodiac, Gemini men fake erections as well.' A triumph of your mind over her matter. You writhe well, your actions are coordinated, you are technically accomplished, but you lack the deep touch that goes into a woman's darkness. You are frequently unable to cast in the long line and trawl her depths. But you chat pleasantly and often heatedly to her corporal assets, and this gives your offers a certain popularity. At your point of crisis one of your personalities may be released and you will find yourself wailing in tune with the familiar rush of pleasure 'Heeeeeeeeere's *Johnny*!'

She never knows when or where you will start, and the uncertainty adds a frisson to your company, particularly in confessionals, in car parks, and around that little spot on her throat just below her ears. Anything can arouse you – lederhosen, kitchen appliances, motorway lights across the harbour. But unfortunately almost anything delivers short-term satisfaction – hitch hikers, cocktail waitresses, gear sticks.

You often need bacon sandwiches and a cab immediately after intercourse.

Deviating

Gemini men can be perverted: freedom of thought and their

attraction to the stage gives them a theatrical perspective on sex, the core of all perversions. The duality of the twins is reflected in the fact that both sadists *and* masochists are drawn to the sign in both capacities. You may be found crouched at WRAF dorm keyholes.

Home

Your deep insecurity frightens you and you may compromise heavily to keep your home intact, going so far as to call your wife 'darling'. However this is only your base and you are generally elsewhere.

Moving house is one of your recreations. You also enjoy minor repairs but you have no stomach for the structural alterations. You have a man do this for you. Often without consulting your marriage partner.

A domineering partner can make you retreat into the privacy of your own thoughts, and this can frighten you. There are things in there that you can't express – you look in *and you know something is going on* – you don't know what it is. This isn't ordinary paranoia. Your partners assume you're on psylocybin, and not without reason when you talk about your fear of being possessed by a demon (Legion, particularly).

Your Little Ones

Others suggest you are not a good parent. You're not. Children get on your nerves after their charm wears off, especially if they aren't talented or attractive. Their single-minded self-interest annoys you, also their way of throwing your present away and treasuring the packaging it came in – you remember being a child, and how intuitively you learned to say what others wanted to hear. Little child minds clinging to routine annoys you too. So you change your instructions frequently to keep them on their toes, and this confuses them. But they like you, even though you lack womanly warmth, especially as a father.

You tell them good stories, full of horror and men without heads.

Women

Strangers wonder where you get your medication. Your fluent speech, hyper-active intellect, soaring cheerfulness remind others of psychiatric out-patients. You are carriers of Filofax fever. All the Mitford sisters appeared to be Geminis, though only Diana (later the prima donna of the British Union of Fascists) actually was.

You make terrifying lady journalists, cool and penetrating – 'Tell our listeners why you wanted to write this contemptible book?' There is a frightening, bird-brightness in your face, a coolness in your clear voice, and you are utterly unintimidated by people's poverty, or social station (though statistically you know a higher proportion of more important people than other signs).

As a competitive humorist you enjoy long rallies, but you can be cruel when the going gets intense, you lose your head and want to win. Your barbed wit sinks in to be removed only with a great deal of mess.

However you are often fair in your judgements – you don't care who is right, because it's always you. You don't approve of idleness and are keen for others to exercise their minds by changing their opinions (generally to yours). You have political skills; you enjoy full consultation (it makes you feel involved), you are best friend to feuds and unhappy families. You despise public service routine which you describe as a mixture of cowardice and idleness.

But It's Not All Good News

In the boiling hive of your brain, plots vie with counter plots. You are skilled at secret operations, making matches, manipulating situations. If you had any purpose in life you would be formidable. Your penetrating mind gathers information, and casts it into wild and attractive patterns, but you generally lack the deep structure to make it mean anything, to transmute the data-base into knowledge.

Reality *bores* you, and you seek escape in fantasy, fanzines utopian politics, organic mescaline – anything that isn't messy with sweat, and sides of beef, and tow-away zones.

This is why your natural habitat is not the countryside. The mud and blood, and the giving birth are all too foul, too fleshy. It has also been proven that far too much of the countryside is far too similar to itself. Fields of wheat back on to fields of barley. In metropolitan life a theatre backs on to a parking yard, which you cross, in front of a pornozine shop into a vacant lot to an Italian sandwich bar to buy two toasted ham and cheese for under a pound – this is what you call useful and interesting scenery.

Nerves Of a Thoroughbred

You are always poised to disappear; your exits are dazzling. You extricate yourself from jobs, opera, love affairs, fist fights, by vanishing. They look and you are not there. You know what time it is in Lisbon and Los Angeles.

You are dangerously susceptible to the glamour of being somewhere else. Because you are reluctant to follow things through your personality spreads sideways. Thus, the more you allow others to know you the greater their impression of apparently unconnected facets, of a serial personality laid out in two dimensions. The orthodox Field Theory that modern physics has given us predicts that you will draw others to you by your (weak) gravitational force, but that the repulsion of your (strong) nuclear force will prevent fusion. And indeed astrological observation bears this out.

You can't live without attention, and are statistically the most frequent suicides in the Zodiac.

In Love

You are skilled at secret operations, strike squads, erotic SWAT teams. Frisky, flirtatious, outstandingly mendacious, you have more friends than is good for you. Your diary has all the precision and intricacy of a medium-sized school timetable. You are tremendously unreliable – even in your deceitful mode you are unpredictable, so spontaneous are you. You hate restrictions, commitments, and quote Blake to justify yourself.

You fascinate a certain sort of man, but it ends in tears (though usually not yours). You have no interest in pain, and are unimpressed with the awful sour-dough honesty others offer you.

What you need is someone with enough money to provide you with psychic space (seven days in Gambia with someone else's water ski instructor counts as psychic space).

Your fear of loneliness (in spite of your popularity, in spite of your multiple personalities you still feel alone in a crowd) is balanced by your fear of intimacy. Together these can drive you into a descending spiral of parties, drugs and unsuitable lovers.

Sexually

You find little pleasure in the flesh. Though you can fornicate quickly and freely, as the Scottish diaries of Gemini Queen Victoria show. You have small aptitude for sensuality, and little physical appetite. You nibble the crudités, you peck at something light, you don't have the Taurean's trencherman attitude to porking up large.

You use sex to release nervous tension, as a displacement activity, to pay for dinner, to take your mind off the television, to defuse an embarrassing situation, for anything but for itself. You are always aware in your intelligent fashion that the purpose of kissing is not pleasure, but to suck bonding chemicals from one another's mouth.

Physical contact is not necessary to you, not for its own sake, not for the sweat and the sex, and the messy beds in the afternoon.

You use sex as evidence.

Evidence that you are attractive, evidence that you actually exist. But be warned that it is not evidence that stands up in court.

Actually Doing It

You can be convincing during sex, as you are a skilful player, like the best bad actors, but you will be caught with your mind wandering. You like to be thought of as sexy and seductive but it is the drama of the act that appeals to you, not the rude mechanical aspects – you like quickies particularly, smash and grab routines, in eccentric places – in express lifts, on mortuary trolleys, in cake mix. In an extended relationship (more than two nights) you will be intimidatingly inventive, and this frightens the opposition. The arrival of your sexual crisis sounds like the Flying Squad.

But Underneath It All

You fear the sense of emptiness which you suspect lies underneath the skin of your personality. This is why you like cigarettes. When the cloud of hot tar globules bursts against your lung it persuades you that you actually have some deep being in there. The journey into the interior is not one you care to make otherwise. There is something down there, and you don't know what it is.

The good stuff comes from deep down. You are often at a loss to get it up. When it does come up by accident, the sudden decompression makes its brain burst at the surface. The mess doesn't help your social life, something you never fully get used to.

The Geminis

Kenny Ball, George Best, Laurence Olivier, Joan Collins, Viscount de L'Isle, Queen Victoria, Bob Dylan, Lech Walensa, Lord Beaverbrook, Miles Davis, Robert Morley, Isadora Duncan, Ian Fleming, John F. Kennedy, Bea Lillie, Bob Hope, G. K. Chesterton, Charles Aznavour, Bernie Taupin, Marius Goring, Anatoli Karpov, Humphrey Lyttleton, Michael McCrum, John Newcombe, Peter Preston, Robert Sangster, James Anderton, Stanley Baxter, Duke of Bedford, Arnold Wesker, Samuel Morse, Ian McKellen, Dave Lee Travis, Jesse Owens, Sir Matt Busby, Peter Cushing, Sir David English, Alec McCowen, the venerable Bede, Cilla Black, Vincent Price, Christopher Lee, Henry Kissinger, Duncan Goodhew, the wholly unmemorable Henry Bellingham M.P., Edward du Cann, Rachel Kempson, Patrick White, Rupert Everett, Nanette Newman, Ray Cooney, Benny Goodman, Mike Todd, Bob Willis, Julian Symons, Clint Eastwood, Denholm Elliot, Terry Waite, Heath Robinson, Prince Rainier of Monaco, Bob Monkhouse, Marilyn Monroe, Colleen McCullough, Gemma Craven, Sir Edward Elgar, Anita Harris, Allen Ginsburg, Margaret Drabble, Ivy Compton-Burnett, Arthur Askey, Bjorn Borg, poor old William Deedes, Robert Powell, Gerald Scarfe, Edward Woodward, John Masefield, Johnny Speight, Charlie Watts, William Douglas-Home, Suzi Quatro, David Hare, Nigel Rees, Tony Richardson, Michael ffolkes, Derek Jewell, Willie John McBride, David Penhaligon, Henry Newbolt, Beau Brummel, Michael Codron, Ray Illingworth, Ossie Clarke, Charles Saatchi, Cole Porter, Duke of Edinburgh, Saul Bellow, Lionel Jeffries, Simon Jenkins, Robert Maxwell, Maurice Sendak, Judy Garland, Jacques Cousteau, Lyndsay de Paul, Athol Fugard, Jackie Stewart, Richard Todd, Ben Jonson, Brigid Brophy, George Bush, Lord Mayhew, Jackie Palo, Anthony Shrimsley, Anthony Eden, Mary Whitehouse, Malcolm McDowell, Thomas Arnold, Julie Felix, Lord Rootes, Burl Ives, Sam Wanamaker, Mike Yarwood and Faith Brown, Richard Baker, Simon Callow and Lewis Collins, Enoch Powell, Erich Segal, James Cameron, Ken Livingstone, Barry Manilow, Lady

Diana Mosley, Beryl Reid, Ian Carmichael, Paul Eddington, Paul McCartney, Linda Thorsen, Charlie 'I Thought He Was Dead' Drake, Salman Rushdie, Duchess of Windsor, Tom Jones, Terence Rattigan, Che Guevara, Anne Frank, Norman Hartnell, Louis Jourdan, and the man with the largest sexual equipment of the twentieth century, Errol Flynn.

CANCER

(22 June – 22 July)

In this, the first wholly neurotic sign of the Zodiac, you sensitive Cancerians find yourselves dominated by deeply damaged emotions. Like psychotics, schizophrenics and random murderers you are ruled by the moon; your sanity goes out with the tide. With some Cancerians the tide is Mediterranean (a six-inch differential), with others it's like Newfoundland (a differential of about fifty-six feet).

The Glyph

Until the early fourth century Cancer used to be represented symbolically by the dung beetle, about which the less said the better. The glyph now has a distant relationship with the Crab. The principle of the sign, so *Woman's Own* tells us, is one of the hard shell outside and being all warm and runny inside, like cheese in a microwave (have you seen Barbara Cartland in her diamante balldress?). Unfortunately, graphic designers have still been unable to represent this in a line drawing.

However, modern astrological research, using many of the techniques developed in NASA's psychological screening for potential astronauts, has shown that the symbol for Cancer represents the structure of a sexual position which is still illegal in many states of America.

The Ruling Planet

You are ruled by the moon – a planet that has been feared, and rightly feared, ever since mankind was clever enough to be frightened of something so far away (not that it is far away; not that it's even a planet, but style matters more than substance to Cancer).

This is the planet of emotion, and strange emotion, dark ideas and turbulent scenes. It turns men into wolves and makes women mad. It is traditionally associated with the night, though astrological analysts still have not been able to isolate the reason for this.

The Karma

Trapped inside or outside your shell you feel your emotions are either unintelligible or overwhelming. Perhaps you have graduated from Gemini or been relegated from Leo. Your karma has been left with an immense emotional apparatus and no mechanisms to control it.

The flood of feeling and the lack of brains give a morbid cast to your incarnation in Cancer. The gulf of dark water below the ice shell. Cancerians feel the blankness of matter, the emptiness of space, the great deserts of silence in the limitless universe, and you rather over-react to it. You seek relief in the shadow-play of emotional life. You generate fantasms and holograms, and they flicker and move against the featureless landscape, under a dull but completely empty sky. Intense, indeed hysterical scenes take your mind off the knowledge that you are going to die, and your flesh will turn to corruption, in the grave, and your soul will fall into this landscape without any furniture to comfort it. It is your task in this life to recognize this, and not to worry about it.

The Personality

For someone as reserved as you are supposed to be, you do allow yourself dramatic changes of mood. You can be taciturn, disagreeable, or manically high spirited – in fact you've got no manners of your own at all (as natural lunatics you don't understand anything that doesn't immediately affect you). But like lunatics you can have insights into others that make you a dangerous companion. You are most communicative in a confessional (with a priest or a psychiatrist) and you are skilled at extracting confessions from others. This has a vital effect on your career in business.

But you remain the same, no matter how the moods move you. The laughing Cancerian is the same as the sour Cancerian – both are deeply, deeply depressed by the cruelty of the karma. This is why you *throw* yourself into things, you throw yourself *at* things too, and this creates bruising. You can often be one of the noisiest signs of the Zodiac, if only to keep back the unbearable weight of silence. This is why you act so vividly, talk so loudly, this is why you attract such hostile glances along the length of the stalls (*Shhhhhhhhh!'*).

You can often be dissociated from your internal machinery, *or* from the effects of your behaviour. You are exo-skeletal. This is the only thing that saves you in society. Your conscious mind scarcely connects with your subconscious – you can exist only in one mode or the other, no useful trade between the two exists. But importantly, the exo-skeleton is mutually protective – not just shielding you from the world, but shielding the world from you.

Your personality is like a great scab covering an active wound. It is a trap over a bottomless well. Into this wound, this well, a limitless amount of other people's sympathy and reassurance can disappear, never to be seen again. Your appetite for kindness is voracious, insatiable, mad. You can drain people, you could drain a whole trainful of people with your melancholy reminiscences of childhood. If you didn't have such a shell no one would dare touch you for fear of becoming immediately bonded to you, as part of a predatory healing process. This explains your often peculiar appearance.

You are a Cardinal sign and need to lead. But if you aren't followed you disappear (many, it must be said, are relieved).

Smart Shell Though

Your need for cover encourages you to hide behind ridiculous accents (Lorraine Chase, Cyril Fletcher), outrageous boastfulness (Colin Welland), or elaborate cosmetic dentistry (Esther Rantzen). It also draws you to jobs or social zones where you can wear a uniform. Thus, many Cancerians are traffic wardens, policemen, commissionaires, soldiers, or Sloanes. But it is disturbing to realize that people who work in uniform are statistically more likely to abuse children sexually than people who do not, and this is not attractive. Only too easily, people become creatures of their uniform. So this tendency should be watched, and often is, and often by the authorities.

Dealing With Disability

Shyness is one of the many defects to which your astrology has condemned you. It gives you an arrogant air (often concealing an inner arrogance at least as strong). This prompts you to disappear abruptly from your midweek dinners at 11.30 p.m. and reappear in your pyjamas, to stand yawning at the door. It surprises those guests you have recently been yelling your party conversation at.

This sort of wild, dislocated behaviour is very Cancerian. For someone who hates the unexpected as much as you it seems extraordinary. But your fear of intimacy is actually a motive force. You are genuinely frightened of people getting close to you (you may catch something). Your sense of hygiene dominates personal relationships.

Thus you can be subject to fairly intense paranoia about the world around you. When the investigators are getting too close you take evasive action – you put on speed and throw your gears into reverse; you go into a slalom at a hundred and ten; you drive over a cliff. You lose them. Whether or not they were investigators. Whether or not they were chasing you. They may not even have seen you until you started behaving in this flamboyantly evasive manner.

And if the moon is waxing, this behaviour is exaggerated.

Violent Reactions

Your powerful grip can be dangerous to those around you, particularly on one side of your body. You get angry too (it's mainly fear) and the powerful, damaged emotion flies around inside your shell like a ricochet. When you get to grips with an enemy you can suddenly flip, and despite your deeply gentle nature you may find yourself dragging his face down a rough-cast wall.

However, your greatest talent remains evasive action. Your dazzling footwork allows you to dodge in and out of contracts (emotional and otherwise). Cancerians are the master and mistress of inadmissible evidence. Everyone knows you're guilty but they just can't get a conviction. Your sense of secrecy is build into your fear for security, and both are strong enough to make you the best spies of the Zodiac, and the best blackmailers.

Nervous Breakdowns

You worry too much, about almost everything. You worry (rightly) about Librans, Aquarians and Geminis. You worry about how to pay your tax, how to pay your accountant and how to eat peas with a fork. You worry about the atmosphere warming, and about the nuclear winter. The American deficit frightens you, low interest rates terrify you. You lie in bed thinking about being attacked by terrorists, being attacked by Mrs Thatcher, being attacked by Japanese competitors.

You're starting to weep a lot, quite often, and though you feel purged by it, it takes more and more tears each time you do it. Perhaps it's your longing for purity and times past. A boy treble singing *Wings of a Dove*, or Bach's painfully sweet, painfully sweet secular cantatas can reduce you to a crying jag. But be careful, there may come a time when you just can't stop: some dyke will be swept down by a Cancerian tide, and you will be taken away. There may be forces you release that you are powerless to control. Be careful, be wary, there are some things that are better left unexpressed.

But Artistic

In the depth of the worst of your moods you long for company. You can't be happy in your misery unless you can make someone else equally miserable. The intensity of this life leads you to make images of it, and stories out of it, and you use these to operate on people you know. 'It's therapy,' they say, 'but is it Art?'

What it is, to you, is some permanence in the mad wrack of time and motion. You generate your own dream world where you can be safe from change. You exist most comfortably in this artificial world to your own design, where everything is processed and ideally packaged.

This hold on death is strong. However hard they try to make you live (see *Tradition*).

Tradition, And Traditionally Tied To The Past

It can't be healthy to be as patriotic as you are. But history represents some security, a safe place for you. At least it can't change, like the present does. All change is decay to the Cancerian: you want to fix yourself in some fortified place (fortified by your favourite things – trust money, dollar investments, negotiable bonds, and an unbreakable marriage contract against your wife – if she leaves you she gets the clothes she walks away in, unless it's fur, in which case she gets nothing at all). Cancerian women fortify themselves against depression by comfort eating (and comfort spending – generally with other people's money – to litter the house with useless durables).

To the Cancerian the past is a permanent thing, and stored in vaults. This suits you very well, incapable of normal life as you are. Possessions are your direct link with the past, and therefore a direct link with your personality – something you need, as you find introspection difficult. Thus your sentimental attachments have the intensity of a fetish. If your house was wrecked by a demolition ball you would suffer a total psychic collapse. Getting the builders in with their sledgehammers can lead to a breakdown. Your home is more than a symbol of your personality, it is an actual *part* of your personality. In exactly the same way that your Cancerian shell protects your soft insides, your house protects your soft outside: your home is itself a sort of exo-skeleton.

Trapped In Your Childhood

Cancerians can be tied to your mothers, and this actually gets sinister, especially to your new bride. It's very late in the twentieth century to be behaving like that. The return to traditional values (like *Psycho*) can be taken too far. It is through your mother that you become aware of your long family history – another particularly unhealthy trait producing far too much snobbery for your social capability.

The fixations stem from an emotional block around the age of 8. The sensitive plates of your mind registered minute sense impressions, and fixed them. They stay with you forever, you remember things indefinitely, which is why the rough passage you had in your early years inflicted permanent damage.

You blame your parents. Your gentle and sensitive nature (you wept a lot and it attracted increasingly adverse comment, particularly through puberty) brought out the worst in your contemporaries. Naturally enough they treated you badly, and your parents failed to provide adequate reassurance (they might have tried but they just didn't have enough to give).

Your anxieties about social relations start here and you never really get over them – these early experiences set up the apparatus for your present dislocations.

You brought it on yourself, of course, the way you behaved with sweets, lending them and charging interest; they didn't like the way you stole from the cloakroom either. No one did, including yourself, but you've conveniently forgotten that; it's perhaps the only thing you have ever forgotten in your life.

Acquisitive, Anal, Mean

You are as tight as a tic, there's no doubting that; even when you pretend to spend nonchalantly you only ever spend nonchalantly on yourself, and a lot of anxiety has gone into the decision. You suffer from a refugee mentality. You know deep down you will never be safe, no matter how big your fridge.

You can just never have enough money, in the same way that you can never have enough love. And you often do things like hide a five gallon drum of water and a case of pilchards in the cellar, in fear of a nuclear strike. You don't hide them from the Russians, but from your spouse who would laugh (they never get used to you, and who can blame them?)

It is all so sad, and self-destructive, because if the bombs don't decimate your assets, capital transfer tax will. The more money you have, the more you fear losing it. The only greater anxiety than saving money, is spending it. It is a game you can't win. The more substantial you grow, the more secure you seem, the more anxious you are. It hardly seems worth it. But money does represent something around which your personality can come out of solution – you crystallize round cash. This is dangerous for you, spiritually, but you can find popularity later in life because of your swollen assets. This isn't all bad (see *Career*).

Career

As a Cardinal sign you know you were always meant for better things – acceptable in a counter clerk, dangerous in a Prime Minister. But you look inside yourself, into the hell of appetite and intuition, and say to yourself, often at the Oscar ceremonies, and often from the podium, 'I've got it, I've really got it, I've really got the goods.' Others recoil when you tell them this, you have to be foxed by alcohol to say it. They remember, and you don't, and you tell them again.

It's just as well that you are usually the employer and not the employed (you are never unemployed). But you are a *demanding* employer, full of a drive to perfection (your subordinates think you are actually insane). But your tight grasp of money, and your intuitive knowledge of what makes a good deal, make you a rich person. If universally disliked.

You started at the bottom and worked up, with a worried expression on your face. Your desk is tidy (sign of a disturbed mind). You are faithful and loyal to your company, and though this holds you back in your career you have a complete understanding of how the company works. As a result when you achieve seniority (you talk about 'being senior' to others) you are consequently impossible. Your understanding of a job description therefore differs from the understanding that the man doing the job has. You finally impress your point of view on him, so effectively that it will leave scars. It's nothing personal, but you feel insulted if they give you less than you expect, you feel scorned, despised. This makes you feel 5 years old again, and you act accordingly. Not a pretty sight but it works.

And of course you understand discipline and take it well. Though this may become unhealthy in your private life, it helps to impress your anally inspired superiors.

Frightening, Too

You can actually be the most intimidating member of the

Zodiac. As a management consultant your greatest talent, as well as your greatest pleasure, is to close unprofitable divisions down. You offer to fire the staff yourself (all of them).

You are a kind man, however, and a decent one, you just like firing people. It's nothing personal, you just feel more secure telling a hundred people to pack their desk and go before lunch. You feel you're dealing and not being dealt to. Which pretty well sums it up.

The Business World's Best Managers

So shrewd are you, so intuitive, that you are terribly, terribly clever with your executives' feelings. You know how to give praise instead of pay, and they never quite work out how you do it. And when you do give pay rises you don't talk in terms of cost-to-the-company but you gross the rise up in tax-terms (you've packaged it to be deductible, to give them the impression it's thirty per cent more than it is).

It is not surprising that Cancerians make the Zodiac's youngest pensioners (private schemes, of course, with a borrow-back facility in which the interest you pay goes back into your own fund).

Cancer is also the sign of working women. Cancerian women get eczema if they don't work. You love your home though, and the thing you love most about it is the woman who comes into iron for you, and clean the bathroom, and cook for the freezer. This may be one of the strongest relationships in your emotional life.

But above all, Cancerian women are respectable workers, and work for respectability. You never star in a suck show, up a flight of stairs, in a bad area. Hardly ever, that is, but pin money is always useful.

Physically

Though you look smart, Cancerians can often suffer from a

critical failure of biological energy in the womb and fail to make the full transition from frogspawn to foetus. The resulting features may be indeterminate – a ledge of flesh for a chin, a soft, smooth, conical head, prone to baldness.

With your eyes shut and your mouth closed you look like a penis in a rather well cut suit.

You may have problems with your stomach (it's so *big*), alimentary canal, breasts and uterus (if female) and mucous membranes (ugh!).

Romantically – Men

You need a lot of love, but you are ill equipped to get it. You never get enough love, you never *can* get enough love. The only thing that loves as much as you need is your mother, and that is no good. Or if it is any good, it's unhealthy.

You need a lot of security as well as a lot of love, and the two just don't go together. With your personality problems you generally get problematical women – really *loopy* birds who are attracted to your exaggerated personality shifts.

The fragile hold you have on yourself (you hold yourself like a teacup, with your little finger cocked) can easily be broken. So can your fragile hold on your lover. You've been going together for nine months, you're thinking of marriage but only too easily she will then do something appalling (laugh through her nose, let her accent drop two sub-classes, blow her nose in her handkerchief and look at the result), and you will go out for cigarettes and never be seen again.

Fearful Emotions

Jealous, possessive, savage you are, and these, women reckon, are your more attractive qualities. You know how to make a woman feel wanted (if she rubs herself against another man at a party you black her eyes – this hurts the woman less than Librans who walk away, feigning indifference).

The toughness of your outer personality causes an extremely complicated refraction of feeling – things come out quite differently from how they went in, and this added to your talent for bizarre dislocations makes it difficult to know what you are feeling about anything. It's safe to assume you are trying to achieve the exact opposite of what you are apparently trying to achieve.

So you get hurt. Well, someone has to get hurt, you reason, but you wonder, in your thirties, why it has to be so unfailingly you.

Your Virginity

Once your affections are fully engaged, once someone has got into your shell, they polarize your sexual being and it happens with an irreversible finality. You are completely organized around them. So sensitive were you, so impressionable, that your submission is complete. You may struggle, feeling that such dominance is unworthy, but Cancerians can only give themselves once. Having done so, you will be preoccupied for the rest of your lives. You will never be able fully to organize yourself around anyone else. Your first marriage will be your only one, no matter how many aisles you travel.

Sexually

Perhaps you actually failed puberty the first time, and had to go back and retake it the following year.

In your early twenties you are not as confident as you might be in matters of sex – also because your body is often a peculiar shape. Other signs abuse alcohol, or solvents, but you abuse dairy products. The fatter you are, the happier; there is a natural sedative in carbohydrates which makes you smile, as well as swell. And you get high on cholesterol. Your love-life often revolves around your stomach.

But you have some understanding of the flesh and your talent for the act grows. Echoes shiver through your sexual element; strange messages sent in some ancient crab-code, some chromosonal vibration giving off information, giving out gene-data, a signal from the interior, like a live quasar out in the gravity fields issuing streams of undecipherable impulses. If you can interpret them you will find something interesting, even exciting, but it will be peculiar. No one else will understand what it is, except the judges you appear before.

Actually Doing It

Even dissociated Cancerians often make the best lovers in the Zodiac combining the liquid dreaminess of Pisceans with the shocking grip of the Scorpio. You mix gentleness with abrasion, and a shocking spikiness in the midst of tender scenes. It is your talent to hurt women and suddenly make it better. You are a dangerous, and dangerously high spirited lover, and during the act of sex you are in touch with yourself in a way you never are when you're sober.

Your deep sense of rhythm helps, and your sexual equipment at certain phases of the moon is more than adequate (if unattractive in the light). Your behaviour in bed may frighten a certain sort of woman, and a certain sort of woman likes you for it. It is an element of menace they find exciting, your deliberate motions and ever-open eyes that add a sinister frisson to your relations. Your sense of the submarine can wrap a woman in warmth. In your late twenties, when you come to know you are rather good at doing it, you can generate the confidence to allow both of you to behave badly.

The least attractive moment in the activity is your crisis, which sounds like a live crayfish going into boiling water.

Women

You weep a lot and abruptly cheer up ('The more you cry the less you pee,' you chirrup) and comforting men are left looking rather silly with their sympathetic faces. You beckon with one hand and threaten with the other, and this confuses those around you. It also confuses yourself, and however definite you appear ('*Someone* has to be definite') your certainties are not based on anything substantial (the moon, the state of your bank account, your weight, your complexion, your sense of grievance all change position daily in your anxiety charts). You change your mind as freely as you change your hat. It is hard for your lover to keep up, and impossible for your husband. Ultimately it ends in disappointment when you're 50 and the children have gone, and you find he gave up trying twenty years ago.

You suffer from a lack, or in some cases a surfeit of intellect: tides run through your mind carrying flotsam which you collect and organize into patterns. Your isolated intuitions make you seem cleverer than you are. You seem to know something about everything, but of course you don't. It doesn't inhibit your definite ideas, and this is why you are never happy with your life, and leave it feeling you could have had a lot more.

Hard To Make Contact With The World

Though you can be intuitive, and skilled with it, this can be a problem. When you put a sequence of furious questions to a man he finds it hard to answer, he steps back with a bewildered expression. When you cross-examine quietly he likes you even less. You put leading questions, and watch him and he comes to understand himself. He resents this technique. He feels he is a part of an experiment, and not a dignified part, on the wrong side of the microscope. It gives him a sense that you don't respect him, which generally you don't, your biggest failing. You actually derive a sense of power from knowing – or seeming to know – more about men than they do themselves, and this is not helpful. You may come to realize this too late in life, and Cancerian women are often found stranded in the middle of a zebra crossing paralysed with guilt.

Deep Down Can Feel Helpless And Fearful

You find it very difficult to ask for what you want, and considering what you do want this is unsurprising. Often you suffer from blocked emotions – the lights change but the traffic doesn't move. You conceal this incapacity by a loud and sarcastic manner – you can have a tongue like a wet towel, and flick the quick of a man. This can make him depressed, at which point you will run out on him (you fear depression like an infectious disease).

Your vulnerability to criticism is extreme (only you are fully aware of how justified the criticism is) but this makes you attractive to intelligent men who like to operate on you.

You feel particularly thin and nervous around the full moon. You will swell and get sexy as it waxes.

The Manipulator

Your sense of control, reserve and progressive profits fit you for management positions, as does your talent for generating dismay. You can circle opponents so quickly they feel surrounded, and when you suddenly go for them they do not know which way to turn.

You appear to be fixed and definite, but what others see in Cancer is not what they get: your talent for disguise and finding cover on thin ground makes it difficult for others ever to catch up with you, and you can lead men astray as they try. You may get a name for this, so you worry in life about your reputation (see *Snobbery*).

The inner turmoil you sense inside yourself leads to a need to try and control life outside, and your efforts to do so result in your unhappiest experiences. The danger that you sense in matters of romance keeps you awake, but once the feeling decays, or matures, into love then you can panic, feeling that you'll never get away, the welding has been too complete. Alas, this panic causes an hysterical lack of action and you find yourself trapped in bad partnerships, bad relationships and semi-detached houses. Your over-developed sense of everything makes you easy meat for cold and rather cruel young men.

Sexually

You retained your virginity long after you had any use for it (you don't like to give anything away), but you need a lot of physical contact, and a lot of money, and this can have an adverse effect on your reputation. During moments of sexual excitement your face swells and darkens, and this can have an adverse effect on your performance in business presentations (approval excites you, budget approval is your highest form of excitement). Your grip is powerful, and painful – you interpret it as fidelity, but you misinterpret.

In spite of your conservative nature, and your overwhelming need for security, you are strangely capable of hit-and-run sex. The weight of your background, your upbringing, your need for security makes it hard for you, but with great effort and application you can succeed in behaving like a slut (but not for long). You don't even feel guilty about it (too guilty about everything else).

In bed this doesn't matter, as alone in the Zodiac with Scorpio you can generate sexual feeling with the intensity of a psychedelic drug experience. When a man enters your element he feels touched as deep as touch goes, and his brain goes off like a light show, his bowels deliquesce (this isn't noticed till later). In the interstices of mind and matter spirit quickens, and in the depth of your sex he feels life breathing, as in the great lung of the world.

The Cancerians

The Princess of Wales, Esther Rantzen, Cyril Fletcher, The Duke of Windsor, Brian Johnston, Fred Hoyle, Laurie Lee, Alan Coren, Helen Keller, Henry VIII, Lord Hunt, Kris Kristofferson, Joe Loss, Prunella Scales, Olivia de Havilland, Debbie Harry,

Lord Beloff, Basil de Ferranti, Lord Home, Ferdinand Mount, Lord Sieff, John Timpson, Stavros Niarchos, Duke of Wellington, Franz Kafka, Joshua Slocum, Prince Michael of Kent, King Taufa'ahau of Tonga, Gina Lollabrigida, Pam Shriver, Neil Simon, Colin Welland, Meryl Streep, Rider Haggard, Jean Anouilh, Adam Faith, Miriam Karlin, Irene Worth, Dr Kinsey, Juan Fangio, George Orwell, Georgie Fame, Colin Wilson, Robert Holmes a'Court, Sir Harold Acton, Joe Gormley, Philip Madoc, P.T. Barnum, Dave Allen, Nancy Reagan, 14th Dalai Lama, Sylvester, Tony Jacklin, Jon Pertwee, Lord Lambton, John Motson, David Hockney, Ian Mikardo, Arthur Ashe, Virgina Wade, Alastair Burnett, Gareth Edwards, Modigliani, Henry Thoreau, Josiah Wedgwood, Moss Evans, Garfield Todd, Ingmar Bergman, Sir William Rees-Mogg, Terry Thomas, Julian Bream, Sir Larry Lamb, Reg Prentice, Ginger Rogers, Wayne Sleep, Ernest Hemingway, Dr Spooner, Charles Parnell, Eric Ambler, Harold Evans, Jack Gold, John Inman, Cyril Smith, Viscount Whitelaw, Jean-Jacques Rousseau, Ian Bannen, Charlotte Bingham, Tony Hatch, Ruskin Spear, Buddy Rich, Lena Horne, Stanley Spencer, Barbara Cartland, George Sand, Leslie Caron, Dr David Owen, Ken Russell, Evelyn Anthony, Dr Barnado, Gertrude Lawrence, Cecil Rhodes, Sarah Siddons, Vladimir Ashkenazy, Bill Oddie, Pierre Cardin, Ringo Starr, Dr Evadne Hinge, Nelson Rockefeller, John D. Rockefeller, Percy Grainger, Mervyn Peake, Marcel Proust, Whistler, Yul Brynner, Julius Caesar, Oscar Hammerstein, Buckminster Fuller, Chris Serle, Norman Tozer, Emily Pankhurst, Iris Murdoch, Julian Bream, Hammond Innes, Lord Northcliffe, Mrs Mary Parkinson, Lorraine Chase, James Cagney, Roy Galton, Tim Brooke Taylor, Dr W. G. Grace, Simon Cadell, Garry Sobers, Dennis Lillee, Ilie Nastase, Catherine Bramwell-Booth, Lord Reith, Diana Rigg, Natalie Wood, Jonathan Miller, Rose Kennedy.

LEO

23 July – 23 August

The lion, and most generally, the rampant lion, like the logo of *The New Avengers*. A great, proud, rearing creature, immensely strong, occasionally dangerous but always terribly, terribly tacky.

The Glyph

In contrast to your sign's aspirations to nobility, the glyph reveals something of your karmic origins, which are low. Few souls choose to come back to earth as a curtain hook – you must have been heavily overdrawn in Aries.

The Ruling Planet

The Sun rules Leo, and what an ebullient ruler it is. The Sun is the planet of shagpile carpet, and driving round Mayfair in convertible cars; of basins of champagne, parties with topless girls *laid on*; condos in Lanzarotte, expense accounts, long lunches, and barging in the stage door, brushing aside the stage manager with the flowers for Lesley Anne Downe ('Have you ever been to the South of France, my dear? I mean *really been* to the South of France?') This is the planet of ridiculous bets to impress girls, of a great deal of noise, of ex-cathedra statements. The Sun is abundant life, overwhelming confidence. The Sun-ruled sign is the spiritual home of bookies, of Jacqueline Onassis, of Mick Jagger, of enthusiastic fornication. Calls come through everywhere for the Sun-ruled – you are always available – having your hair done, at the gym, at lunch, in your car – telephones ring for you when you are in the lavatory and you answer. It makes you feel wanted.

The Karma

Your past lives have been spent as some form of highly developed earthworm. You have drunk deep of humility and solitude. This is why you now appear in the party-pack version, the economy size, telling jokes in the centre of a crowd of people, arm wrestling all-comers and doing coin tricks. 'All right everyone, gather round me!' you call, making the field signal (cocked hand on crown of head) that scoutmasters use. You are generally to be found at the centre of a crowd of people, attracted by your loud voice and fat wallet (it isn't fat for long). Your karmic mission (you usually decide not to accept it) is to realize that success is an illusion and security a vain ambition. Like a Bolton boy who has known poverty and horror in his childhood, you drive yourself to the top. This is why when you put on your crashing telephone voice it sounds like an American 'dewing an Inglish arcksent'.

The Personality, Men and Women

You have an ego as big as a basketball, and you bounce it around without worrying whose face gets in the way. Natural leadership is your primary quality, you feel, so much so that you fill this in on census forms and passport applications, even when it isn't asked for. No matter what size you actually are, you seem bigger. You inflate your chest, you blow out your stomach (your Leonine diet sees to this), and in later life you can sit around in front of *Match of the Day*, in your yellow sweater like a condom full of custard.

The social authority you appear to have is often an illusion – a victory of style over substance: Mick Jagger at the Altamont concert ('Hey, cool it, okay, we can have a beautiful time, stop pushing at the back, okay, *cool* it okay:'). Leo Willie Rushton can also make a living as a comedian without being funny. On the other hand there is Leo Bernard Manning ('There's a Jap in the audience! *Pearl Harbor! Pearl Harbor!* Here – you look like a nice young lad – piss on that Jap!')

You always know better than everyone else, and even when you don't your opinion feels weightier than theirs. Part of the reason is your posture, which is that of a dress sergeant. Benito Mussolini had the Leonine physique, though every time he broke wind his chest sagged, a common problem for Leos. You are particularly impressive when you marry rich men (Jackie Onassis) but you can degenerate into a fatal matiness to keep in touch from the centre of attention (Barry Norman). In either case you justify your preposterous behaviour with a charming smile and the phrase, 'Well, hey, that's the kind of guy I am.'

You are absurdly susceptible to flattery – it has the force of an uppercut on you. Appeals to your charity often work, appeals to your generosity generally work, but appeals to your vanity go straight to your head and from there to your heart. For this reason you are far more easily manipulated than tighter, meaner, more anal signs like Virgo and Capricorn – a trait that makes you socially indispensable – everyone should have a Leo they can practise on.

You love being indispensable. This is why you will do anything for anyone who asks properly (they have to call you Godfather). You will do anything to extend your influence, your involvement, for you keep a fairly detailed table of accounts, and there comes a time when you will call favours in, particularly when you get older. You use your indispensability as a career tool, always looking for a way in to any situation, which can seem at odds with your regimental dignity – largely because it *is* at odds with it. But it does allow the flow of some sort of emotion – you big Greek clown, you oral indulgent over-consumer, you big, warm, sloppy wally.

This excellent opinion you have of yourself makes you vulnerable to satire, and women, and clever little academics who duck the full blast of your authority and come in under your guard, weasling. Luckily your vulnerability is obvious to everyone except yourself, so it simply doesn't matter – no matter how you are despised it is a social rule that people take Leos more or less on their own terms.

This is just as well as you have no interest in disapproval; it is a waste of energy and you do not encourage it. You are boastfully intolerant of disagreement, let alone disapproval: 'I think that's a pretty well discredited idea by now, isn't it?' and 'Fuck off you little sod or I'll pull out your lungs,' are two statements you often make – indeed some Leos say little else.

Street Behaviour

You are a popular metropolitan sight, driving your Bentley round like a film producer, sounding off about how vulgarity causes you actual physical distress. You wrap your large boastful body around people, and those who don't know you may object. You stand in the street with a big look on your face, and everyone has to walk round you.

Leos are an ornament to any city, with your day-glo taste in colours, your big-chested blondes, your stereo distorting when you pull up at the lights (you often change the tape from Buck's Fizz to Bach, to make a better impression on the pedestrians).

You intervene in brawls on the tube, and often you survive.

Loud In Indian Restaurants

Leo's spiritual home is Manchester, but you come down to London for the money and fame, where you give too much of 'that' (you wag four flat fingers from the mouth), and not enough of 'that' (a bunched fist is pushed rudely up to shoulder level, and your mouth twists, yob-wise). You call Indian waiters 'darkie', you greet friends with 'What's yellow and sleeps alone?'*, and you talk indefatiguably about 'totty *gagging* for it'. You also love practical jokes – you pick up someone's dinner in a restaurant and throw it at them, you drop a cockroach down a fat woman's cleavage, you hide a leper in your best friend's linen basket.

Therefore it is one of the deepest mysteries of the Zodiac why this sign does better for air stewardesses, women journalists, minor models and Jenny Agutter than any other sign. Your fear of infection is the only brake on your indiscriminate social relations.

Tremendous Bores

With your big, bluff, reassuring presence you are very often quite wrong (the declaration of the First World War) – but you are so certain you often get away with it. This costs a great deal of money in the end.

Your overspending, your domineering generosity, your inflexible need to have everything your own way also wears down your friends (or if friends is too strong a word, your collaborators). No wonder they keep refilling George Melly's glass, they're terribly keen for him to pass out so someone else can get a word in.

The joke is you never do pass out. You simply keep talking, long past the time anyone can understand what your thick, twisting tongue is trying to say.

But Attractively Volatile

Leos often enjoy cheerful explosions of brainless rage. It clears the air. Only in afflicted examples do you attempt cosmetic

* Yoko Ono

surgery with a tyre iron. But it is the heat of the moment that produces this behaviour, Leos can't carry grudges (you haven't the concentration). Leo Fidel Castro recently gave an old university friend a ten-year jail sentence for 'failing to greet him with sufficient enthusiasm'. If Castro is true to his astrology he very probably won't make him serve the full sentence, or if he does, it will be not through malice, but because he has just forgotten about the whole incident.

Wisdom And Strength

Leos want to wield influence (like Jonathan Dimbleby), to talk very loudly and carry a baseball bat. You have, both men and women, a masculine nature. One which (feminists say) is a female nature that has aborted at the gene stage, a semi-evolved creature, unable to see anything except in terms of your own self-interest.

But ruthless self-interest is not uncommon in the Zodiac, and at least you want other signs along for company, if in subordinate roles. And there is an ebullience in your combination punches which can often be exhilarating for admiring signs.

But Not Competitive

Technically you are not competitive because you don't compete. Robert Mitchum, for instance, could hardly be called competitive. You assume you are the leader. If this is disputed you simply don't play. You take your basketball ego with you and sit by yourself for up to fifty years.

In fact you have to win everything you do – score the most goals, most girls, most pints of beer. You can't keep your dignity without winning. If you don't win you don't survive. Now, it would appear that a personality like yours could take a lot of punishment and still smile, but this is not the case. Your spirits visibly revive when they let you get ahead. The sulky look on your face when the opposition rooks get in amongst your second-rank pawns is so awful that they often let you win just to wipe your face clean.

Social Misfits

Leos often start out life;

in a row of terraced houses, with the pit in spitting distance;

in a tower block in Bermondsey where the level of urine in the lifts licks at the deckled ledge on the uppers of your semi-brogues;

on an estate in Chingford with petty criminals and van drivers and printer's assistants and yobs on corners hanging out for change;

in Manchester.

Leos feel they were meant for better things – Leo women particularly can be awful hell like this (that *telephone voice*!). But Leo men, though you can do well, though you can do well enough to spend £22,000 a year on lunch, yet you are still handicapped by the fact that when you put on a dinner jacket you look like a boxing promoter.

The Child Within

You were often treated well as a child, and this has had awful repercussions on your adult life (if you can properly be said to have an adult life), or for those that let you share their adult life. Your tantrums were effective then, and they can be twice as effective now that you're three times the size.

If squashed at an early age you may appear less ebullient than you should. However, when your spouse discovers the Leo talent, she will think you have been possessed by a demon. It will also worry your colleagues: what they see is not what is inside. You may appear calm and authoritative, self-controlled, but inside is some were-animal which can come tearing out through the flesh when aroused beyond restraint – it makes a dreadful mess of the loose covers, no less than of your marriage.

The Tragedy Of It All

But every Leo, except the obvious ones, simply does not get away with it. Your parents start the long, attritional process of socializing you ('You're not the only person in the world you know'). Your teachers drive home the advantage; ('Yes, yes, all right let someone else have a go now.') Your girlfriends jump on the wagon, ('Show some respect! *Don't*! What do you think you take me for?') And your wife delivers the monthly coup de grace, ('You sodding great pig, you make me *sick*, do you hear, physically *sick*!')

It bears down on you over the years. Your vitality may sink into some hole. But however humbled, however humiliated by life, your pride is still down there, in the dark, biding its time (which may never come). You can be very depressed for years, without ever really knowing it. So depressed you may go out rallying at weekends.

No one with real self-confidence behaves as noisily as you do. What is it that you are secretly afraid of? Not being liked? That should be a real fear for you. The suspicion of some dangerous haemorrhage deep down certainly operates on your astrology as it operated on Lawrence of Arabia's, the Queen of the Desert. If only he had been better liked he wouldn't have behaved in so outrageous a way, and neither, probably, would you.

Romantically, Men

Anyone who needs as much affection as you do is romantically active, though few signs are so active with so many. Where you get them from is a mystery, as you need very specific females: girls who are immune to embarrassment, for instance. Girls who admire you for your extroversion, the singing in the street, the tipping Athenaeum staff, the shouting at friends on the other side of the road – girls who glow at your shoulder with the energy you let off: there aren't many girls like that in any one place, but what there are, you find. Some defect, some open wound in their psyches draw them to you – girls who lack some vital confidence, girls who feel a need to be connected to the great gay world, girls who don't have any money. You find them in bars, at parties, on buses, in a way that virtually no other sign of the Zodiac can. You are always on the lookout for girls. Balzac wrote nearly a hundred novels simply because he didn't do anything else in life. You are the same with totty (it's your word, totty; 'Cop for totty, did you, Sat'd'y?').

You prefer shopgirls and legal secretaries, and defective Sloanes (though all Sloanes are defective), and girls with big round eyes who look at you with unmixed admiration (you don't know much about girls but you know what you like). They relax in your big, enveloping warmth (never a good thing) and soon they are chatting away. You often have to be quite firm with them before they sit smiling while you chat away.

In the course of your romances your credit cards take a frightful beating. Your generosity is unconditional, and you often fail to land the fish you hook – she takes the bait, the line and the solid silver lure and you never see her again. If you do meet her again you may beat her with your credit cards, show *her*.

But once you've got one she is very much yours, until you move on. You plaster yourself all over the relationship, like Polyfilla. You take power of attorney over her opinions, and this makes both of you happy (so peculiar are Leos' women). You finish her sentences, and order her dinner, you speak for both of you, even to the marriage guidance counsellor ('Yes, yes, all right, let someone else have a go,' you tell him).

Sexually, Men

You are sexually over-active and the wild oats you sow can be measured in imperial pints – you have an enormous appetite for new flesh. You perform so vigorously that girls complain about the smell of burning rubber after going with you, and the long ache below the waist: they feel they've been in a car-crash. You are one of the great sexual soloists, and often you come to a climax with the exuberant vocalization 'We are the champions!'

A Phallocrat

You get in quickly, often on the first night, like some big animal. You press women against walls and put your hands under their buttocks, lifting them off their feet, 'You bitch,' you say to them, 'you don't know what sex is!' *And they believe you!* You have what women like – an unflawed sexual confidence and a penis like a beam engine. You will allow her no quarter, no privacy, you want possession of her mind (with the sort of women you usually get it is vacant possession).

The Unintelligible Words

When girls refuse to go to bed with you you claim you can't understand what they mean. 'Take your clothes off,' you say, 'let's go for a good time, doll,' or even, 'Come on darling, you know you love it.'

They turn you down and you say afterwards, 'I heard the words but I didn't understand what they meant, I tried, but I couldn't see what she was trying to say.' And what happened then? 'Oh we went back to her place, she was gagging for it.'

Actually Doing It

You bear down on naked women, often from behind, and bite their necks. Your musk overwhelms them and their eyes roll back in their heads so they cannot see your hands which are busy about their declivities, diving in and around them while your flesh communicates its warmth. You bring women to the boil in a way that they like, grappling with them, pinning them to your limbs, forcing yourself between their knees. You hold both little wrists in one large hand and interfere with her with the other – all done with growls and bare teeth and a sob at the back of the throat. You also make sudden autocratic demands: 'Bend over! Eat the carpet! Bring in your friend!'

You really wreck the bed.

Your technique includes much penetrative variation, and you often go on and on, even when your partner is tired and disinclined. Post-coitally you have two very effective technical tricks. You either fall asleep immediately on top of her *or* you fall asleep immediately, wrapping her in your big cuddling arms until she can't breathe. This way she calls herself a cab in ten minutes, the first way gets you a beer and a bacon sandwich in ten minutes.

Dealing With Him

Unfortunately, the Leo's blood pressure is rarely high enough to inflate his enormous organ (and when it is high enough he gets a heart attack). His only sexual vulnerability is to flattery – 'You don't need a condom you need a rubbish bag' is the most effective. With flattery you cannot go over the top. The Leo will believe anything at all.

Maritally

Man and wife are one person, and that person is the Leo.

The battle for the *maistrie*, the mastery, the upper hand can still flail up some interest in the art of marriage (the way you practise it, it looks like boxing) even after some years, but aimiable sloth takes its toll on the Leo, and you are content to survey your shrinking empire with equable good humour. Minor irritations (Virgoans, possibly) are useful to keep you interested in life, but domesticity will generally reduce your ambitions to *Match Of The Day* and a six-pack. Ultimately it turns out that your greatest marital talent is carpentry.

For the greatest success in married life you need a woman who is not only gratefully inferior to you (there are few of these), but also one who will stay gratefully inferior (there are none of these at all). However, you will always do well maritally while you can cast your wife in leading roles (Blake Edwards is happily married, if only to Julie Andrews).

Your Career

Your biggest character defect that goes down on your evaluation file is your habit of framing *and hanging* pictures of yourself taken with socially significant personalities.

You are a *pushy* employee, who believes he can do anything ('The first rule of show business, kid,' you tell anyone who'll listen, 'is never say No'). The principle is good, but it gets you into a lot of trouble as you are rarely good enough to deliver on your wilder promises. You solve problems by taking them aside and kicking them till they die ('You may not like me, but you've got to admit I'm effective'). Your employers put up with you (new business presentations find you at your most intolerable, and most effective. So does lunch, and you do best in professions where personality is more important than talent – publishing, producing TV shows, writing screenplays). You have ideas too, and if encouraged you will invariably be unsuccessful, breaking up under the weight of vast entrepreneurial schemes. You do well as a fraudulent executive, conscious of your status more than anything else in the business: your secretary phones his secretary, you're both on the line but neither of you will be the first to speak. Neither do you ever agree with anyone in an argument. You take up your position and let no one else on board while you assault every other position in the room: for every victory there can only be one victor.

But you cut a fine dash in Jermyn Street with your newly fashionable trilby, and the velvet-collared astrakhan. Though you do draw the sarcasms of scaffolding workers ('Fire a rivet gun at the silly sod').

You are mechanically literate but take no pleasure in anything except charging for your services (you commonly own highly profitable garages).

Women

Other signs say, incorrectly, that they would know exactly how to spend a million pounds. You know exactly how you would spend a million pounds in three weeks. You have no interest in purity and poverty. You need a lot of grooming, a lot of looking after, you are a high-maintenance item. Leo women have to be cherished, complimented and made exceptionally comfortable. There is often a deep lack of security in you, and it is this which is fed by excessive attention. Men can pour compliments into your head as though down a drain.

You are rarely intelligent. Very often you have the brain of a small soap-dish, but you are proud of it. You even boast of it. 'I may have the brain of a small soap-dish, but I know What Really Matters' (drinks parties, white weddings, public schools).

You are an astonishing cliché of a woman, and it wouldn't matter unless you were so loud, so proud of it. You need a strong man, a dress allowance and something of your very own to smack (babies possibly). As a mother you will spoil your children (they are half yours genetically), but also discipline them fiercely (half the genes are someone else's). You would give them a tougher time but your attention span isn't long enough.

Socially

You are quite good at snobbery, and quite pleased when people tell you so. You scowl at vulgarity, but are surprisingly coarse within yourself. You can be oafish, especially when drunk, and especially with jokes.

One of your major drives is to get *out* of the house and *into* society – you are run on a comfortable budget of high-tab dinners and big denomination money, and very expensive cars (gallons to the mile in town). Sex on impact is not impossible for the ambitious Leo (Enid Blyton had an early reputation for leaving teeth marks in the wallets of randy Lamborghini-driving Levantines), but it is a social rather than a sexual relationship. Similarly Leo women in wicked stockings are happy to take a taxi across London, naked in a fur coat, just for the fun of it.

Women like you too, but they occasionally slip their hands into your bikini bottom which rarely makes a good impression on you – and never makes a good impression on Princess Margaret whose Leonine qualities certainly don't include bi-sexuality, not even on Mustique.

The best theatre for your talents is the bedroom, and you feel best sitting up in bed with a dozen young men looking at you from the chaise-longue. You may be eating chocolates. No one else will be talking except to urge you to more speech, and more chocolate.

You look best, socially, naked but for your tiara. You blossom in front of the camera. Men talk to you about your career (they find it is the fastest way to see you naked). You make a good impression when you bring your legs along, and a better one walking down the hall in nothing but your high heels and hairstyle. This is the one sight in the Zodiac it is worth risking a major coronary embolism for.

Maritally

Marriage is a terrible disappointment for you. The things men will say to get you into bed are far less deceptive than what they say to get you into the matrimonial bed. Once in the deep silence of that pit you will sense with a sudden chill how little his performance will match up to his promises.

Without regular application of uninterrupted sexual intercourse you Leo women go cold. You direct all energy away from sexual centres and divert it into your hairstyle; you become dissociated from your sex life and never find it again. Excessive promiscuity can have the same effect, so try not to appear virtuous simply because you've been without communion for four years.

Anorexia is always an option (especially with your dieting problem – you can't diet) though you still like to eat a lot. You often throw up between the brandy and the bill. And so practised are you that you can do it silently – possibly your most impressive technical accomplishment.

You also ask ridiculous, unanswerable questions like, 'How *dare* you speak to me like that?'

Sexually

You don't mind whether men are particularly good looking but they must be big.

You have had many sexual associates; the value of your sexual stock is high – animal grace is considered your best feature by your keeper. And you keep records of the transactions, sensing that your children will need something to corroborate your claims, when you are 50, that you were once able to inspire affection and even desire.

You may appear shy at first, but with very little encouragement you get into your stride. This may surprise many men. Your mouth is generally open (you can't keep quiet for long) and the teeth that are bared may alarm the same men who have just been surprised. They only get actually frightened at your climax which can have all the passion of a shark attack – the poor fellows have a very real sense of being ingested.

Deviating

Anything which pays you excessive attention interests you – threesomes in which you take the starring part, cinematography, interrogation scenes where you are the one strapped to the chair (you need a spotlight and more than one interrogator). You can take either role, active or passive, depending on which is more centre-stage. You would star in a vegetable revue if asked by an attractive-enough producer.

Important For Men

Do not complain. *Do not* explain. *Do not* apologize.

The Leos

Princess Margaret, Mussolini, Mick Jagger, the Queen Mother, Milton Friedman, Alexandre Dumas, Robert Graves, George Bernard Shaw, Richard Ingrams, Princess Anne, Carl Jung, Blake Edwards, Stanley Kubrick, Lionel Bart, Alan Whicker, Robert Holmes à Court, Shirley Williams, Jackie Onassis, Clive Sinclair, Henry Ford, Geraldine Chaplin, Jonathan Dimbleby, Marina Ogilvy, Herman Melville, Yves St Laurent, Viktor Korchnoi, David Essex, Michael Foot, Charles Hambro, Amelia Earhart, Sir David Napley, Thomas À Kempis, Susan George, Vitas Gerulaitis, Lance Percival, Lord Thorneycroft, Clement Attlee, Haile Selassie, Hilaire Belloc, Sir Karl Popper, Sir Garry Sobers, John Stonehouse, Nigel Aspinall, Lord Scarman, Lord Grimond, Paul Anka, Peter Bogdanovich, Kate Bush, C. Northcote Parkinson, Peter Nichols, the third battle of Ypres, Laurie Taylor, Ossie Ardiles, Jack Straw, Stanley Baldwin, Georgina Hale, the declaration of the First World War, Alan Hoard, Chris Bonnington, Frank Finlay, Dom Mintoff, Alfred, Lord Tennyson, Greg Chappell, Kenneth Kendall, Mata Hari, Sir Joseph Cantley, Connie Stevens, Rod Laver, Izaak Walton, Eddie Fisher, Anna Massey, Norris McWhirter, Fidel Castro, Buddy

Greco, Robert Bolt, Jim Dale, Sir Kenneth Newman, Napoleon Bonaparte, Thomas de Quincey, Menachem Begin, Ted Hughes, Tom Maschler, Trevor McDonald, Robert de Niro, George Melly, V. S. Naipaul, Ginger Baker, Arthur Calder Marshall, Sid Going, Dame Janet Baker, Diana Churchill, Len Murray, Peter O'Toole, Terry Wogan, Myrna Loy, Anthony Sampson, Rupert Brooke, Tony Bennett, Shelley, Neil Armstrong, Sir Freddie Laker, Lucille Ball, Barbara Windsor, Andy Warhol, Robert Mitchum, Dornford Yates, Dustin Hoffman, Philip Larkin, Ian Anderson, Enid Blyton, Angus Wilson, Alex Hailey, George IV, Cecil B. de Mille, Sir Alfred Hitchcock, Annie Oakley, Bernard Manning, Rod Hull, John Galsworthy, Sir Walter Scott, Lawrence of Arabia, Wendy Hiller, Julia Child, Georgette Heyer, Mae West, Rosalynn Carter, Robert Redford, Shelley Winters, Willie Rushton, Madame du Barry, Ogden Nash, Jacqueline Susann, H. P. Lovecraft, Jim Reeves, Count Basie, Lord Goodman, *Barry Norman*, Honor Blackman, Steve Davis, Dorothy Parker, Ray Bradbury, Debussy, Coral Browne.

VIRGO

24 August – 23 September

Many observers of the cultural scene are still unaware of why they never quite like Patrick Mower; or why they find Roald Dahl's short stories rather long for their length; or why Dame Judith Hart (her politics aside) is the last woman you'd want to share a sauna with; or why Ian McGregor is so pathetically vulnerable on television; or what that something is around the mouth of Derek Nimmo that is so repulsive.

The answer lies in the fact they are all Virgoans, or as modern astrologers now say, anal.

Virgoans, locked out in the astrological suburbs, have had an undeservedly bad press. It's not a pleasant job, but *someone's* got to do it. What other explanation is there for John Peel, or Henry Ford II, or Lady Antonia Pinter?

Your Karma

No sign is more bound to the Wheel Of Life than Virgo. This is the sign of separate cheques in restaurants ('Now, you had coffee but you didn't have dessert, so your bill comes to . . .'). You have chosen this incarnation to learn that the material world is not worth the idolatry you lavish on it. You have come down to reform your cosmic attitude to housework, food processors and BMWs (you are *for* them, and no one should be so certain about anything as you are about this). But more importantly, you have come down to work on your attitude to knowledge – not just O levels but to the Cosmos itself.

In this incarnation ('A long life and a grey one') you will be taught by dust and disappointment that there is more to living than thinking. You will explore the limits of reason, logic, intellectual achievement and find they don't give you enough real satisfaction. You will come to feel the deadliness of the clichés in which you express yourself: you will probably never overcome the certainty that you are more correct than your fellows: these are the illusions you have been sent down to address.

You Can't Break Out

There is an essential virginity about the Virgoan. It is a membrane which separates you from experience, a membrane which prevents you from reaching out and making contact with the mess of the material world; a membrane which allows you space and peace for mental detachment (Peter Sellers), but which may end up suffocating you (Caligula). Dry cleaners print warnings on their poly jacket bags: keep membranes away from Virgoans and children under 3.

A Negative, Feminine Sign

You are astrologically associated with fussiness, cleanliness, and unsparing personal criticism. These characteristics have traditionally been associated with Larry Grayson (a classic Virgoan type) and married women. However, the American philosopher Valerie Solonas (who subsequently shot Andy Warhol) has this to say:

> Being an incomplete female the male spends his life attempting to become female. He attempts to do this by constantly seeking out, fraternizing with, and trying to live through the female and by claiming as his own all female characteristics – emotional strength and independence, forcefulness, dynamism, decisiveness, coolness, objectivity, assertiveness, courage, integrity, vitality, intensity, depth of character, grooviness *(sic)* etc. – and projecting on to women all male traits – vanity, frivolity, triviality, weakness etc . . . The male claim that females find fulfillment through motherhood and sexuality reflects what males think they'd find fulfilling if they were females.

This talented, if radical, philosopher bases her most profound insights on the datum that 'Deep down, every man knows he is a worthless piece of shit', which shifts discipline from metaphysical astrology to anal hygiene – another strongly Virgoan sphere of interest.

Your Personality

Captain Bligh was the Virgoan most sailors admire most. Naval discipline is a strong point of this sun sign, and Virgoans are unable to enjoy themselves, even on drugs. Prince Albert was the classic Virgoan, and the classic consort – it was to his relief that he did not live long.

Virgoans hate vulgarity, but because you are dissociated from the world you have little taste of your own. You can be seen wearing cravats. You can even be seen wearing leather trousers saying, 'It's an amazing job I have, because it's just such an amazingly cool organization to work for.' When you put on a dinner jacket you look like a snooker player (Mother Teresa is a rare Virgoan exception to this rule).

Indifferent to central heating, you Virgoans put up with it for the sake of your domestic partners – this is the sign of Young Fogies and the Methodist Labour Party – conceited self-sacrifice is what you do best, the production and distribution of guilt via your own moral superiority is your primary industry. You can offer a great deal of advice (Glyn Worsnip, J.B. Priestley and Violet Carson, Confucius, and the aptly named Black Rod, Lieutenant General Horrocks) which no one takes. 'If I were you–' you say. 'Thank God you're not,' they reply. Your small, anal gestures reveal your inability to reach through the membrane that separates man from humanity. Part of the reason for your imprisonment is the fact that you nurse grudges, resentments. You store them, as in a battery. The more grudges you have, the more substantial you feel – your first and most major mistake. However, those close to you often do not pick this up: your highly educated exterior hides your personality flaws from everyone except the person you're married to. You firmly believe in the superiority of your talent, your perceptions, your graceful syntax. This may be true for Virgoans living below the Tropic of Cancer where there is also some understanding of sex. It is not true for Ian McGregor in Bolton. It is occasionally true for Jimmy Young on Radio 2 (but only since 1981). Valentino was a Virgoan, but then it was demonstrated in his autopsy that he owned one of the smallest recorded *membrum viriles*, and that the redeployment of his blood supply meant he suffered from impotence whenever he blushed.

You Virgoans are ruthless self-improvers, but your bowels are subject to blockage. William Wilberforce, who took all the credit for abolishing slavery (very Virgoan), suffered from stools like combustible briquettes.

The Scientific Mind

As a material idolator you have no faith in anything you can't see, can't feel, or can't predict. For this reason you can be profoundly stupid. Your sharp intellect deceives you. You cannot conceive of anything since classical physics (Newton is – 'still *perfectly* serviceable! It was Newton's physics that put men on the moon!' – rather than the great Piscean Einstein's, let alone Bohr's). But though you claim for yourself a scientific mind (you are often very sharp, and very clear-sighted), it is more the mind of an engineer, a laboratory technician's mind, the mind of a scientific grammarian, an educated grocer. Your major talent is to obstruct the imagination of wild young men. You are the engineer who jeers at the scientist, the scientist who jeers at the particle physicist, the physicist who jeers at the quantum philosopher, the philosopher who jeers at the mystic. You betray yourself with your fondness for knock-down arguments and regular boastful appeals to 'get your heads out of cloud-cuckoo land'. For this reason Virgoans tend to make good technicians, statisticians, engineers and book-keepers, but not very brilliant scientists. You are crippled by common sense. Your view of reality is too three-dimensional.

You Virgoans have to be carried to a conclusion because you can't see the destination for the detail. There is an awful pedestrian inevitability to your thinking process, a dogged onwardness which you pursue to the central meaninglessness of your view of the world.

Because you can't make anything of modern physics, you still see the universe as a great clockwork machine – regular, predictable, mechanical. You view Newton's achievement as a triumph of enlightenment: it was his theory of gravitation that released man's intellectual energies from the straitjacket of superstitious Christian feudalism. To your great relief everything became mathematically exact, express, predictable, a common-sense universe which obeyed laws that could be explained at O level.

The bleak philosophy of determinism which results from this (there is no free will in a clockwork machine – it can only run down) is rather to your taste. You can enthusiastically subscribe to the meaningless of life, the emptiness of the universe, the insignificant part played by mankind, the insect mentality of his trivial civilization. It's partly philosophy, and partly the influence of your anal hygiene fetish. For Virgoans like Dorothy Parker this is hardly surprising. It cheers you up to jeer at the nebulous self-deceptions of woolly minded crypto-religious Piscean types.

However, it is important for you to realize this: when you

look at the world and see an intricate, accurate machine – useful but basically dead – *you are casting the world in your own image.*

Virgoan Threats

'I'd wipe that smirk *off* your face if I were you.'

'I suppose you're finding this amusing at the moment. Well, you'll be laughing on the other side of your face before I've finished, let me assure you of *that*!'

'If one of you doesn't own up the whole lot of you will suffer.'

But It's Not All Good News

Your adverbs are neatly, methodically, precisely, fastidiously. That is how you do things. Virgoan Bernie Winters' big, sloppy mouth is ruled by a different ascendant. You rise early and work late, in spite of the effect this has on your digestion. You are wonderfully diligent, but it takes its toll on you in this careless world: you build physical defects (especially your own) into a general theory about the decline of quality. This is accurate but unattractive – no one wants to hear the Virgoan Savonarola recastigating the twentieth century for its design flaws – a reluctance you file under design flaws. (By the way, note the etymological correspondence between Savonarola with the French for 'soap' – Virgoans are obsessively hygienic, see what Lee Kuan Yew has done to Singapore).

Sharp Tongues

Which are not popular with the opposite sex, especially at times of intimate contact. Everything has its place and if you Virgoans don't remind your friends of this you will get sick. Your tremendous conceitedness means you cannot resist criticism – you cannot take it, but you cannot resist making it.

It's not a question of tact but of aesthetics – your stomach clutches you when you leave ugliness untouched; a character covered with eggstains cries out for the Dabitoff of your personal interest.

Your own appearance is an example to us all, at least all of us anal-retentive, hi-gloss, socially ambitious flagellation fans. Your blazer and grey flannels assume a moral significance: when you see *deliberate* scruffiness (it's not clever *or* amusing), you feel it is an attack on all the things that make civilized life worthwhile (blazers, flannels, absence of *deliberate* scruffiness). This chimes happily with the times, as the conjunction of Saturn and Pluto, which began in 1982 and will last for thirty-three years, is promising a time of increasingly collective values, which under Mrs Thatcher is a very strong mandate for blazers and flannels. As opposed to Mr Kinnock's rude-boy jeans and camouflage jackets from Millets.

However, do remember from blazers and flannels it is a small step to a penchant for uniforms so you should be wary: there is a statistical relationship between men who work in uniform and men who sexually abuse children (see Cancer).

It Appears We Have A Humorist Among Us

Your highly developed sense of personal hygiene suits you for work in the satirical field (the filth in your face and on the streets of London enlivens your active glands). Novelist Martin Amis, the *enfant horrible* of metropolitan literature, exercises his Virgoan genius with a density of disgust that surprises even Virgoans. ('With her clothes off there was no reason to suppose she would smell of boiled eggs and dead babies').

D.H. Lawrence, also undervalued for his sense of humour, was similarly stimulated by 'the impure, the foetid, the death-seeking flesh-filth of corrupt and putrefying brain semen'. John Betjeman, another son of Virgo, took a more moderate view, owing to the lack of coal-caked sexual savages in the hip baths of his childhood.

Perhaps it is your wide-eyed innocence that helps you in

your satirical career; that sense of virginity, of naivety, of watching from the comfortable side of the membrane, which makes it so difficult for you to understand how people can behave as they do – the theft, the rape, the blood and the horror, the plunder, the mindless violence, the destruction of souls – and that's just how you describe the first year of marriage.

You can do without it, life in the Crush Bar, leave out the sharp elbows and the awful women shrieking at each other from different entrances; big, wet fools behind their enormous bellies, smelly women, and foreigners with foul breath eating sweat sandwiches – ugh! You're glad you have no real part of it, content to watch it on the closed circuit monitors.

Note: A large vocabulary is an oft-found trait in this star sign. Jean Luis Borges, who hasn't made a joke in his entire literary career, has one of the largest vocabularies in South America.

Your Major Talent

Is queueing. And you often join the longest queue in the Post Office, arguing that there must be some good reason for the other queues being shorter. The truth is that you just find safety in numbers, and initiative makes you anxious.

However, Virgoans can often appear highly intelligent (Raquel Welch, Lady Antonia), particularly to yourselves. You have the ability to judge relations between things, you enjoy metaphysical poetry (especially when it isn't metaphysical), you are often the cleverest boy in the class ('We don't set much store on *cleverness* at Albion House'). You have tremendous aptitude for classifying, codifying, spying on your neighbours and putting it all into files. You often become authors as a result.

Sadly, though, you lack body (but not bottom, you often have more bottom than you want). You lack passion. Like Bob Newhart you would be no match for a stupid, powerful woman. Your protests sound effeminate and you are easily defeated. Though you will never give in you may still be overwhelmed. We are surprised to find Lord Weidenfeld in this company – his struggle against his astrology has been both long and brave.

Your Career

This is the sign of petty officials and small executives. Too busy to be successful, too worried to work to the top, too literal to be tactful. You are a diligent and productive hack. Depending on where you start in life you may find it difficult to reach the very top – there are so many grades to work through – unlike Librans, who vault their way into high office. You will succeed through, if you don't switch disciplines. You may make it to the top of your division, or in exceptional cases the division above you, if you start early and work late. You are generally short of money. The problem is not that your wife spends too much, it's that you don't earn enough.

Your conscientiousness, attention to detail and sheer professionalism will earn you the hatred of your subordinates (Sam Goldwyn, in spite of the sheer professionalism of his success, was consistently voted the Most Unpopular Employer Of The Year by the seven trade associations), and though you will please your superiors you will probably bore them too. Be wary of asking them home to meet your wife. If she's another Virgoan you will be marked unfit for promotion. If she's not, your superiors will try and go to bed with her. If your attenuated sex drive has left her *gagging* for it, many may succeed.

Others are arrogant because they are unsure of themselves. You are arrogant because you are arrogant. And why shouldn't you be? Someone has to stand up for quality. And look at the large number of O levels you have! Notwithstanding this you prize stupidity – 'The egg-headed boffins in the back room might be amused by this so-called *book*, but I'm afraid to say that I can't claim to be a pseudo-intellectual, I'm awfully sorry.' You shrink from university educated women, as if before a cross.

However, you do have a talent for cobbling together compromises at the office – your belief in reason means you want everyone to be happy, and that there are sensible answers to everything, and if everyone could just address the problem rationally for a moment something can be worked out. This basic fallacy holds you back in your career as fools and bullies elbow you out of the way with their superior strength and nastiness. Virgoans can sulk, or nag, or make snide suggestions to get your own way, but you rarely dare to lash out with a lance of simple power to impose your will. The spontaneity frightens you. So you hide behind a mealy reasonableness. This serves you well in the long run – you may never do brilliantly but you will generally do well. You would much rather be a living mediocrity than a dead genius.

You are best as uncreative accountants, car mechanics (though your instinct for honest invoices is a handicap), engineers, classical physicists, quite good doctors, snooker players (you enjoy the anal display), ironists, novelists, and practical inventors (you manufactured the first washing machine).

But finally the sad fact is that you can never really to places without two jobs – something the man born under Virgo simply cannot cope with. Two jobs makes the Virgoan brain explode.

Virgoan Parents

It is a universally recognized truth in the parenting fraternity that the children should outnumber the mother and father. However Virgo's small, obsessive handwriting is mirrored in his small, obsessive family units.

You make remote fathers, but not remote enough for your children, whom you embarrass by turning up at the school wearing a cravat. Your respect for authority makes you feckless in front of their Housemaster and invisible in front of the Head. Your submissive posture does none of you credit. Even though you have come to complain about the bullying and the beating (not enough of it for your taste), you can only pass anodyne sarcasms about the central heating.

You have what appears to be a cold and suspicious nature. Neither are you inclined to display affection. Deep down, though, like all authoritarians you are very sentimental and you love dogs, babies, and girls in fluffy sweaters (until they all get streaming diarrhoea).

Things Virgoans Know

It's a long life and a grey one.

There will be tears before teatime.

It's later than we think.

You have to be cruel to be kind.

Houses do not clean themselves.

You have to get the dirty water off your chest.

The sins you do by two and two ye must pay for one by one.

There's no need to inflict your grief on people at funerals – it's unnecessary.

By giving money to Ethiopia you destroy their local markets.

In Love

This is not a natural state for you, and frequently leads to your brain bursting, like a water filled condom-bomb. After the first rush of love and sex and horror you fall away, appalled at the mess. You go home for a few days to collect yourself – your lover feels abandoned and betrayed and never forgives you. But you had to catch up on your correspondence which is important to you. Sir Rupert Hart-Davis is Virgoan, but not a very good one, judging from the letters he published.

You can sometimes feel inadequate (largely because you are inadequate) with no idea of what to say or do, even when it is a simple matter of putting your arms round someone and whispering that everything's going to be all right (the physicallity of the action is profoundly upsetting for Virgoans). If your love affair goes well (fat chance) you may be able to make your partner feel comfortable – like a first-rate air steward in Club Class – but you will *rarely* make her actually happy.

Virgoans have few real love affairs, except with yourselves (Virgoan Jimmy Connors pelvic display on winning a point), though you are keen for love, especially for social advancement. You are too picky, too hygienic, the grid that women have to pass through has a very fine mesh. Fastidious, clean, reserved, you may be attracted to many women, but something at the last minute (her laugh, her fat lower lip, her habit of scratching) will make her repulsive to you and you'll leave her bewildered. You are rarely jealous, largely because you rarely give enough of yourself to be hurt (you look on it as squandering your emotional capital).

Emotional honesty is a cross you have to bear – you pare, refine, examine, search closely for the truth. But you do this without warmth or charity, and though it may be useful it is too technical to be attractive. It doesn't bring you closer to others, examining them in this way, it does the opposite. You talk your emotions out, as it were objectively – what a profound lie this is – and yet your skill is to do it so reasonably that it is hard to see the fear underlying it ('If I were to ask you to marry me/come to bed with me/go out to dinner with me, what would your response to such a category of question be?').

You can have a rare talent for gallantry (a concealed acting ability showing through) as long as it doesn't tear your clothes or make you dirty.

Trying To Get Him Into Bed

The Virgoan is not susceptible to sex or glamour. He likes girls with sensible shoes and plaid skirts with a large safety pin in them. Don't look as though you enjoy a good time, do not be pleasure-seeking, don't ask for drugs, don't get drunk, don't talk to strange men at a party (he will assume he can't compete and he's probably right).

Never walk in on a Virgoan when he is sitting on the lavatory. Even though he spends a large part of his recreational time there he is sensitive about it. Much of his early potty training (which amounted to anal violation) has been responsible for his personality problems, so be aware that in the lavatory you are approaching the core of his being. If it should happen that you do break in on him, pretend it never happened – he may well go into hysterical amnesia and forget about it. If you refer to it he may kill you.

Virgoan Sexuality

Your precise diction, retentive memory and sharp tongue lead many of your friends to assume you are basically homosexual. This doubt makes you question what you do, often while you are doing it, and this is not satisfactory for either of you. Your basic instinct is for chastity, or at least for celibacy (you can't keep your hands off yourself), and you approve in principle of the Hindu concept of Kundalini, a spiritual snake of retained semen that grows up the inside of the spine.

So you are never able to crush your partner against the wall and growl in her ear *'You bitch, you love it'*, never grip her buttocks and haul her up into your groin, never throw her down on the bed and shove her face into the pillow. And this is a shame because many women enjoy this sort of thing, if only for a change. However, you like to wear washing-up gloves during sex, and this may excite dormant streaks in some. You considerately maintain silence during sexual intercourse as you cannot think of anything truthful to say, and many women are grateful for your restraint.

Actually Doing It

It is unreasonable to suppose that Virgoan men do not engage in sexual intercourse, but the evidence of contact is getting slighter and slighter in successive sexual-astrological surveys. The increasing incidence of crippling venereal infections has severely inhibited the hygiene-conscious Virgoan. As a final phase in a courtship Virgoans are known to conduct an obstetrical examination of their partner prior to first coition, using surgical gloves and a beef extract compound (the salt stings any open lesions). Full sexual relations are aborted at this stage ('What's the matter?' you call after her angrily, 'What have I said *now?*')

However, when relations do occur after a long series of conceited meetings in upwardly mobile Perrier bars (your sex drive is intimately linked with your social ambitions), you may find yourself drunk enough to find a man to take you home. The fact is that Virgoans simply are not immensely interested in hetero-sex, you are far more interested in uncomplicated orgasms.

Too precise to be passionate, too self-conscious to be abandoned, you make a polite, efficient, goal-oriented performer, more interested in orgasms than in sex itself. And in spite of the homosexual connotation you can be popular with efficient, goal-oriented women. You are considerate, and democratic as well, anxious to make her comfortable, much like that first-rate air steward, and you wait as long as you can for her to catch up. You dutifully play around with her, as sensitively as you can, but when she makes those light little gasps you don't know whether it is through pleasure or pain, and you don't actually care except insofar as it reflects on you. The only noise you make during the act tends to be little panting signals that your crisis is approaching (the noise is to alert your partner to a need for urgency). You take the weight on your elbows, and generally assume the dominant role, though with some diffidence. Your hands play over your partner's body with a light touch ('It's like being in bed with a lot of insects,' one woman married to a Virgoan reports). This can be exciting for those who admire gentleness and restraint. However, women who want to be crushed, women who want to feel their ribs creak as you grip them, women who want fusion, and eruption, and *filthy* things to be growled in their ears, Country and Western women find you a pretty thin soup.

Your sex life is like your traffic life: you are a careful driver and you raise the standard of manners in the road – you let people in ahead of you, you slow down when they overtake you, you'll even talk to them on your CB. The one thing you won't do is let them drive your car.

Deviating

Your favourite perversion lies in the area of corporal punishment. You can spent a significant proportion of your sexual vitality on magazines portraying schoolgirls having their bottoms smacked. The theatricality of flagellation appeals to you, no less than the pain (Virgoans find pain much more reliable than pleasure). However, you must be aware that the act of flagellation has very little to do with sex as such. The connection between such pictures and the ecstatic union that sexual intercourse represents is remote. This deep-seated desire for submission, mastery, and blood-speckled birch weals makes satisfactory relations rare. Even when pursued with a willing partner the sexual results are curiously unsatisfying. Oh well, you say, never mind, there's more to life than old S–E–X.

And When It's All Over

Virgoans will be astonished at a woman's lack of dignity, her blubbing face and blotchy skin as she pleads with you not to go. You fold and refold your hands wondering when you can politely plead the last train. You sit there quietly, among all the marriage smelt that's been drained off, wondering why everything has to be so messy. In the end you are happier by yourselves where you are surer of controlling the situation.

Or When Virgoans Get Married

Marriage is slightly less unpleasant to the Virgoan than being in love, so you will ultimately accept it. The sooner the better, as emotional plaque builds up very quickly, and a bachelor Virgoan approaching 40 needs very unusual women – either one skilled in sandblasting, or one naïve enough to take you completely on your own terms. Anyway, from what you've heard about marriage you fear it more than a strip-search at customs. Certainly the probing, the penetrating, the absolute lack of privacy make the first year hell. It is the most upsetting change of life since you were sent away to prep school.

However, you are constant in love, and have a well-developed streak of domesticity. In all unimportant matters – the washing-up, the household insurance, the regular salary, you excel. And neither will you sink into the sofa with a six pack and *Match Of The Day*. You have every chance of happiness. This is because you can supply the thing that wives want most, more than a four-figure dress allowance and continental shoes: what wives want is *sacrifice*, and sacrifice is what you do best – though you are careful not to suffer in silence.

Women

There's something touchingly vulnerable about Virgoan women. The only thing that will love you as you want to be loved is your dog.

Loyal, efficient, successful and self-sufficient though you may be, yet your deep lack of confidence makes all your high critical abilities rather pathetic.

It is your respect for authority that makes you so vulnerable to our pity. Countess Spencer is born under this sign, which explains her hunger for authority. Any representative of a larger body (London Transport, head waiters, underground guards) forces Virgoans to bob into a submissive posture. You feel yourself to be very low on the food-chain. You look so vulnerable sitting upright on the tube, with your hands folded in your lap, wearing the fawn coat you ordered from the back of the *Daily Telegraph*. You would do anything a man in a white coat told you to, *any*thing.

Your caution is that of a terribly small, shy person. Low self-esteem makes you dangerous. Much of your barbed wit comes from this deep feeling of inferiority. You can never accept a compliment ('Oh what? This old thing?'), never relax with your position in the world ('*Why* will people not listen to what I tell them?'), never give yourself freely ('Yes make love to me quickly, and then buy me a dishwasher').

You are the sign that is least accessible to human intercourse, and the most feminine. You buy creamed corn in the mini-mart, you make beef-boil-in-a-bag for lunch, you work cotton buds into places no other signs know about, you straighten pictures and pick lint from folds in your partner's flesh. Are these feminine qualities? Valerie Solonas labels them masculine, in which case you are the most masculine. The Virgoan Queen Elizabeth I was probably neither. Like Russell Harty. Shirley 'Superwoman' Conran is probably both.

On the good side, your low self-image keeps you out of the way. Though it does encourage you to write a great many novels – Agatha Christie, Mary Renault, Antonia Pinter. On the bad side it makes you demanding, nervous, critical. 'I'm only being practical,' you say, as you wind up for a meticulous inventory of missed appointments, sloppy dressing, grammatical errors, dirty fingernails, cheque-stub inconsistencies, thoughtlessness, carelessness and general attitude. You are acutely aware of these things and your protestant ethics, no less than your ruling planet Mercury, encourage you to get your retaliation in first; 'constructive criticism', Virgoan Ena Sharples called it. But unlike Aquarians, you tend to keep your sharp tongue to yourself until you are at very close quarters with others, and this is something to be grateful for. However, when you are at close quarters you can be lethal – author and gardener Beverly Nicholls, the *Daily Express* tells us (Virgoan newspaper), actually tried to kill her father because of his unhygienic habits.

You are diligent in the home (no one has any cause to lay blame on *your* stoop), but you will not dress chickens for roasting because they look like babies. You are economical to run, though you occasionally allow yourself to look ridiculous (using the Harrods carrier bag for shopping in Watford). There is a streak of ruthlessness in you too. You will wash spiders down the plughole, and though you know, deep down, that this kills them you say cheerfully, 'Spiders live in drains, that's how they come into the bath in the first place, it doesn't harm them a bit!' When you say such things your elevator doesn't always seem to go to the top floor.

Romantically

Love doesn't come easy. When you fall you take care not to let anyone know, particularly the object of your love – he wouldn't want you to, it would only embarrass you both, it probably would never have worked anyway. Thus you prefer impossible lovers – married men with children, homosexuals, terminal patients.

Nor does love go easily either. You keep all the lost love you can, for old times sake. New partners feel there is a third party in the room with you both.

You don't really want to be loved. You want someone you can respect to take you into service.

Sexually

Sexual activity finds you at your loneliest. You find it so hard to reach through the membrane and make contact. Tension may inflict vaginismus on you, alcohol will only make you quarrelsome. You make a distant lover, but compliant. If he really wants to do anything you may well let him, particularly if it seems the thing to do, even if you don't like it. It is part of your nature to improve your technique in everything you do, driving to making love. You try to improve but men are so strange, so quick, and built so small that you wonder whether there is something wrong in you (it may well be that there is). You also need a great deal of solicitude, perhaps too much of it. He must undress you himself, something he never enjoys doing, but otherwise you will do it in the bathroom, and take so long that he'll doze off over a book; you slip into bed in a towel, with your knickers on, for modesty's sake. This is a good start, but you must be prepared to take the knickers off, before you want to, if necessary. It is a busy world we live in, and you must respect business timetables. You take longer to get under way than almost any other sign – it is not unusual to take four days of uninterrupted sexual intercourse to bring you to a crisis. He needs to wrap you in himself, soak you in the solution of his sexual being, envelop you in warmth and confidence. In this atmosphere you may blossom, make your needs known, make small little panting cries, and whimper, regress to babyhood, take on masochistic qualities, ask to have your bottom smacked: it's such a relief to have someone else taking all the responsibility. However it is humiliating when he tells you not to be perverted (perhaps you should stick to sex with your own sign – the guilt is part of the enjoyment). Also you don't like him to perform oral sex on you as you feel isolated up there with no one covering your nakedness.

Afterwards you may say either 'I feel like a whore,' or, 'Tell me a story.'

Questions The Virgo Asks

What if everyone behaved as they wanted to?

But how did you ever let yourself get *in*to this situation?

Why does that jolly phone go as soon as you get into the bath?

The Larger Areas Of Concern

You worry about law and order (not enough of it), students urinating in doorways (too many by half), the increase in violent crime (too steep), liberal intellectuals (too shallow). You are the sign of pre-Suez England, when there was still some respect in the world, some idealism, some concern for quality. Back to basics, you say, head out of the clouds.

However your main and abiding concern is your worry that people don't respect you enough – your many talents (queueing, book keeping, writing letters to newspapers about the three Rs) are undervalued. It's not a pleasant job, after all, and *someone's* got to do it.

Of Course You Make The Best Automata

It is for these reasons that you, in common with Taureans, make the best Nazis.

The Virgoan traits – respect for authority, idealism in the matter of hygiene (especially anal or racial purity), fussiness with detail, obsessively tidy fingernails – add up to an accurate inventory of the authoritarian personality. Hegel himself, the inventor of the Nation State, was, significantly, born under this sign. His interest in corporal punishment was also extreme, even for a philosopher.

But where Taureans serve to form the great amorphous mass of the Nazi powerbase, Virgoans, with their typical delicacy (you don't care for the vulgarity of the mob) rise to be SS majors, administrators, interrogators (you use hatpins). There is a profound sense of bureaucracy at the heart of the Nazi. You identify with the neat solutions offered and the vision of a well-ordered society, a disciplined workforce and chastened children. Routine marks out the rhythm of your life, giving it meaning and tradition. You fear your own spontaneity, so of course spontaneity in society makes you anxious. This trait goes through the Virgoan personality as a unifying principle –

it connects your deep fears with your view of society and physics.

The Virgoans

Jimmy Young, Ian McGregor, Upton Sinclair, Larry Grayson, Russell Harty, Lady Diana Cooper, Sophia Loren, Twiggy, Mungo Park, John Dankworth, William Golding, Pete Murray, Derek Nimmo, Martin Amis, Jeremy Irons, Zandra Rhodes, Russ Abbott, Lee Kuan Yew, Dame Judith Hart, Stirling Moss, Roddy McDowell, Junius Jayewardene, Anne Bancroft, Sir Alexander Korda, B.B. King, Charles Haughey, Peter Falk, George Chakiris, Agatha Christie, Greta Garbo, Nichol Williamson, Lady Soames, Margaret Lockwood, Lord Cobbold, Amanda Barrie, J.B. Priestley, Lord Weidenfeld, Roald Dahl, Maurice Chevalier, Angus Ogilvy, Patrick Mower, Kenneth Lo, Freddie Jones, Maria Aitken, D.H. Lawrence, Sir Patrick Mayhew, Judy Geeson, Jose Feliciano, William Bligh, Cardinal Richelieu, Topol, Countess Spencer, Michael Frayn, Noel Barber, Siegfried Sassoon, Jack Rosenthal, Sir Harry Secombe, Britt Ekland, Malcolm Bradbury, Bernie Winters, Pauline Collins, Malcolm Allison, Jesse James, Lord Delfont, Raquel Welch, Lady Antonia Pinter, Henry Ford II, Dinsdale Landen, Lord George-Brown, Jimmy Connors, Charles Douglas Home, Cecil Parkinson, Lord King of Wartnaby (*where?*), Evelyn de Rothschild, Ernest Rutherford, Caligula, Clive Lloyd, Garry Sobers, Sir Bernard Lovell, Roy Castle, John Peel, Jonathan Aitken, Dana, Denis Healey, Countess of Longford, Sir Peter Parker, James Hunt, Elliot Gould, Christopher Isherwood, Sir Rupert Hart-Davis, Hegel, Confucius, Bryan Organ, and obviously, Sir Basil Smallpiece.

LIBRA

24 September – 23 October

Libra is Greek for weight, and Libran women worry about this, and with cause. For all the suffering and death in the Zodiac, the anxieties of you Libran women all stem from the fear that your bottoms are too fat. Libra is also the chemical parent of Librium, which every Libran needs, and often in massive doses, depending on which amazingly ambitious career phase you are moving through right now.

The Glyph

Though conventional scientists still favour the interpretation of Libra's glyph as that of the scales, which are the scales of justice, the scales of cocaine dealers, the scales of bisexuals (you dip both ways), yet modern astrologers now believe the glyph to be an architectural elevation drawing of Brigitte Bardot sunbathing.

The scale motif is not, in fact, appropriate as modern research has shown Libra to be the most wildly unbalanced sign of the Zodiac.

The Karma

You have been made aware, half-way through your karmic journey through the Zodiac, that there is a world beyond the world outside yourself, a world where all apparent contradictions are made whole. Your soul is now grown up enough to recognize the interdependence of good and evil. You seek to reconcile the eternal polarities of the universe, your yin and yang, your masculine and feminine, your cheque stubs and your bank statements. Of course it can't be done, not in this country, but you are ambitious. Frighteningly ambitious.

In all your endeavours you long for fame and admiration, and this is spiritually fatal. So we see Clive James abandoning his early promise to become a sort of witty Denis Nordern. Mrs Thatcher invades the Falklands. Jimmy Carter becomes President of the United States.

You can veer wildly from one extreme to the other (you call it research, because that's tax deductible). It can be financially fatal too, when the Revenue queries the legitimacy of your cocaine deductions, and ask for receipts (you oblige).

Your Ruling Planet

Venus is a lot of trouble, the most obvious light in the evening sky, heading for the horizon, which is America, heading for those restaurants where the menu has big tasselled knouts hanging from it and you give the maitre d' $200 for a table by the window; nothing but the best for Venus. The influence of this planet is powerful, stimulating desires for Bentleys, Vermeers, and uninterrupted sexual intercourse. Marketing men love Venus, she is the patron saint of the energetic consumer. She is the planet of kitchen acquisitions – love, sex, food processors, being taken roughly from behind over the washing-up. Venus puts her hair up, Venus sits naked at her dressing table powdering her body with a big fluffy puff – no wonder Libran men (Jan née James Morris for instance) have a peculiar reputation. There is some artistic talent here (which can only confirm the peculiar reputation).

The Personality

This Mental – Air sign produces representatives who are gay, witty, diplomatic and charming. These are recognized as your most irritating traits, especially by your wife whom you belabour with your charm, though not your gaiety (she won't let you). She finds it bad enough when you operate on her, but when she sees it working so easily on strangers she wants to be sick (if she's Aquarian she probably will be sick, if she's Sagittarian she'll probably be sick over your head).

Your astrology is firm on the subject of these sociable qualities, yet you are a nightmare to live with – you make no distinction between public and private debate, and you frequently address the dinner table with rhetoric, as though it were a delegation. If you are Libran Sir Michael Edwardes it probably is a delegation, even if it is your family.

Few signs are as bad tempered as yours (Nietzsche, F. Scott Fitzgerald, Jeremy Isaacs) and this makes people laugh – though often your gaiety, wit, diplomacy and charm are most exercised in public and your comic explosions of irritability happen alone with your already dangerous spouse. Other signs may be moody, but you are mean with your moodiness and have a talent for nastiness that surprises those who know you slightly (i.e. everyone). You can swear fluently, and with a vitality that frightens your family. And you often have absurdly curly hair, except for the sleek Librans who do not.

Librans love fine things, beautiful furniture, old paintings, and you draw strength from them (though not when they belong to someone else). You are the most ambitious sign of the Zodiac – you need not just material goods, but also the admiration of the many, the adoration of the few and a Bentley. So gay, witty, diplomatic and charming are you that you rarely succeed in this.

Libra's Incredible Lack of Balance

It is true that Librans seek calm, peace and harmony, but only as a method of getting everything your own way.

You join arguments on the losing side. You respond to the weak (not because you sympathize with them, but because you hate to see bullies bullying – in fact anyone getting their own way, other than yourself, arouses your pugnacity. You love arguing (one of your most basic drives arises from your belief that you know better than anyone else) and your nostrils flare: it shows how agile you are, how supple, how attractive. You are always in the minority, where you are most visible.

If you were actually interested in harmony rather than showing off, you would not behave with this manic extremity: you try and jump the Grand Canyon on a rocket-powered motorcycle, you drink too much and stay up too late, and when you get maudlin you call Pan Am and book a ticket to L.A. to try and get Ricki Lee Jones into bed. This is not how reasonable people behave. It never works.

If you really were a balanced individual your wife wouldn't have to ask you to do the opposite of what she wanted whenever she wanted anything.

Sane, Though Neurotically Sane

You are not unstable, but you are unpredictable. Two days after you move house you are figuring out how to subdivide and move out at a profit (this is true of your marriage too). You have a horror of finality. It's not that you're unstable, you just can't bear to be pinned down. And actually you are pretty unstable. You watch Jan Leeming reading the news of horror and abduction, and that sob at the bottom of her larynx makes you cry. The chorister singing Lloyd Webber's *Piè Jesu* makes you cry. The full orchestral version of *Rule Britannia* makes you cry. This is not stable behaviour.

Your reputation in the Zodiac for sanity, neutrality and

balance is inspired by your practice of joining the losing side (and what could be more neurotic than that?).

The House Of Partnerships

Though you are subject to fits of panic, the Seventh House, which Libra represents, is the house of mutual cooperation. You do not do well as a lonely figure in a landscape, you need an audience. But remember you are also a Cardinal House, and this means that no matter how much consultation you take, or how much attention you pay to the views of others, finally you have everything exactly your own way (Mrs Thatcher, again, Christopher Booker, Melvyn Bragg, Robert Muldoon, Heinrich Himmler).

As a partner you can be intimidating – the energy you have is astonishing, the work you get through is amazing, and you hate contradiction. You dismiss objections to your new ideas with ruthless vigour, especially old fools saying there must be a reason why such a thing hasn't been done already – 'It hasn't been done because nobody's thought of it before, or if it has been done before then it shows there's a market for it, and if it has been done before and didn't work then it shows it wasn't done properly.'

Much of your energy is spent in bringing a team together, matching the complementary skills of two people to make a power-four. One of the people is generally yourself: though the fact that you are invigorated by argument does not make you a partner that other partners feel particularly comfortable with. You work like an amphetamine-inspired Jap and then collapse like a clothes-horse. But even then you are at your most alive when your partner cannot answer you; you generally behave as though you have been abusing cocaine, and this has a morbid effect on your popularity.

Bewilderment and disappointment follow the break-up of your mutual endeavours, but you survive the bruised look of your former colleagues: 'Don't worry about that,' you say when you meet the deadbeats on the street, 'listen, I've got this great idea . . .'

Socially

You are continually available for social intercourse, practically anywhere with practically anyone. You concentrate steadily on others. This cannot be healthy. Too much is going out and not enough coming in. It is your principle to scatter, not hoard, and though this may make you more attractive, it also makes you poor in substance. Certainly in your twenties you are feckless enough to be trapped by bores, and you make weak leaving noises as you hover round the door for forty minutes, weeping with frustration. In your thirties you develop a ruthlessness (talking very loudly, bouncing back the boredom, walking through the door, looking at your watch and still talking) which helps you in your life's work of getting your own way in everything you do.

Your agility with language allows you to tease, to penetrate, to say breath-takingly intimate things without appearing personal or impertinent. 'What sort of noise do duchesses make when they climax?' you ask a duchess. Though often you do appear personal, and impertinent, particularly in your twenties, and particularly to duchesses, and they dislike you for it. It puts a limit on your ambitions, certainly until you learn restraint (often you never do).

Others must realize that you need to be settled before you become trustworthy. You need a house, a family, an enthusiastically supportive wife ('Gosh, that's probably right darling, you know, I never thought of it like that before') – fat chance; your intense social ambition must be stilled; your erratic nature must be organized round some useful activity (*not* looking for God, or yourself), very probably making money – a surprise for the sensitive, artistics wimps so many Librans can be. Even then your friends and family will watch for your restlessness to come round again, as it will, with the spring.

You are incapable of keeping a secret until you grow up (around age 35).

Part of this insecurity comes from the same source as your need to talk so much. You feel you are insubstantial. You feel you are very little there. You are driven to talk in order to give evidence for your existence. However gross you appear, you fear the wet, bloody experience of life; you can't take it untrimmed of its fat, running with oils and grease, spluttering and jumping in the pan. You react better to elegant abstractions, to colours high in the electromagnetic spectrum, it's Bach you like, and expressing human relations in graceful algebraic equations. The intractability of the material world is a disappointment to you, though you love to watch women backing into too small a parking space.

Chess is as close as you care to come to real gore. You combine a street fighter's aggression (you hate street fights) with an abstract, problem-solving ability to be an excellent low board chess player. You hate losing so much (the humiliation is crushing) that you concentrate on your losing positions with an intensity that makes you win, simply by will-power. You are good enough at the game to believe that no one can be genuinely intelligent without being good at chess.

Advanced Management Techniques

You are sensitive to the needs and fears of other people, and this helps productivity. Much as you hate any kind of emotional disturbance, you have found over the years that people behave significantly better if you shout at them.

They may not like you immediately, but they will immediately respect you, and Librans are the fastest sign in the Zodiac to convert respect into affection (so magnanimous in victory, so vicious in defeat). This is not to say that your tantrums aren't serious. You often mean them, and retaliation against you is found to be unwise. You can lose yourself for hours in dreams of revenge. Indeed, your major creativity goes into schemes to humiliate your enemies in front of your friends.

Are You Indecisive?

If your emotions aren't engaged (usually they are not, you're pretty cool customer, as you like to say of yourself), you can happily agree with both sides. So you get a reputation for crawling, but this really isn't justified. But your ability to take up contrary positions gives you insights into all oppositions (you may end up a transvestite as a result) and you are naturally good at finding common ground between factions (there's no need to look so pleased, they despise you for it).

However, when you have an interest in the outcome your impartiality vanishes. Your decision is quick and forceful, like mortar fire. Many suffer as a result, especially when you're right.

But like Mrs Thatcher you can take too much advice. On your best behaviour you do want everyone to like you (a very dangerous idea), so everyone has their say. Everyone except the miners. And Cheltenham GCHQ. But practically everyone else, unless they're in the Cabinet. Cleverly though, your invisible influence can weigh in an employee's discussion, manipulating their views round to discrediting these strategies and promoting those. Your colleagues have to resign themselves to their karma – they can do anything they please, but it won't affect the outcome.

Sensitive, Artistic

So sensitive, in fact, that you recoil from the sight of a man in a traffic jam with his finger sunk up to the first joint in his nostril. This is only one of the things you cannot bear to witness – there are many others (see *Women*). Your insecurities stem from your sensitive nature – you were probably damaged in childhood by some brutal experience of the world (cowboy films, Catholic schools, altar boys, being dropped on your head) and this can give you a faintly startled look in later life.

You can suffer from sudden headaches. Some cerebral overcrowding makes it feel as though you've been punched in the brain, as though someone's slipped a shiv into your eye from behind. You generally look happy, but the smile doesn't always go up to your eyes. This may be why, but is probably not.

Many Librans have a theatrical ability, in and out of the theatre. For this reason you are often smart dressers, though you can be absurdly taken up with Hobbits (wearing an awful duffle hood), or religion (priests' coats buttoned from the throat to the groin), or Sloane girls (studded wrist bands, they like it rough, you surmise, and you're wrong). However, for all your dramatic abilities in making people feel sorry for you, you are too tense to show anything real of yourself. It even takes you up to twelve rehearsals to lay a message on your answering machine.

In Your Career

You are helped in your career by having ideas well above your station. Your ambitions are not always impossible (owning own home, buying a dog, getting married), but the wildness that is an essential part of your astrology can make it more difficult for you than for others.

You can be undirected. There is so much happening in your brain – marketing ideas, musicals, diving lessons, girls, hangovers, colour schemes, design templates, pending patents – that you can be little aware of what is happening around you. You never deliver on a contract until the last moment. Your employers can never count on a contract until you've signed and returned it. More than any other sign you go up to the bedroom for the iron, and come down with the laundry, wondering what it was you went up to the bedroom for. You can just get away with it at home, but the board doesn't like it when you are summing up your division's annual performance.

Your career can include a life sentence in an executive prison, because if anyone tries to cheat you out of money, you will kill them. This is your most endearing characteristic – one of the few times we see deeply personal behaviour expressed – if it weren't for this habit of homicide it would be impossible to get close to you at all. Anyway, your sympathies are instinctively with the criminal rather than the victim – there's something so shabby about being a victim, especially when they're physically damaged. This attitude has the most positive effect on your career – your superiors warm to you for it.

You need an agreeable work-station too, with tubular effects, and lacquered desks, and clean, pleasing colours. Librans do not do well in steel foundries, where your co-workers regard you as a poof and try to melt you.

Librans make sensitive servants – you work hard and can subsume your difficult personality into your master's, or your spouse's. This is the only way happiness lies for you, though there will be little success in it, which is why you never do it.

Romantically

You are the most talented flirt in the Zodiac. You cannot meet a woman – unless a *real* dog – without wondering whether you want to sleep with her. It is a sign of your overwhelming conceit that you never wonder whether she wants to sleep with you – this is one of the reasons you are not more successful with women. Just one of them. Generous-minded friends say that you confuse love and friendship, but the truth is you're a slut.

As a talented communicator you are clever enough to look into the opposite sex and throw switches in there. You can't bear to be ignored, so you behave as an attractive and amusing person, as you've found this to be a good way of focusing attention on you. It works, but it also ends in tears.

You have strong morals, but they don't stop you doing what you want to do. Ideal morals, strong but elastic, they can be stretched like lycra into a transparent figure-hugging gossamer. You also have a great sense of humour which nine out of ten women say is so important (it is important, but only if you have no sex appeal – and anyway, Librans perversely go for the tenth woman who thinks a sense of humour is as important as a sense of humus). But of course you love to laugh, and loudly. It's what you're good at, though your strangely bleak view of life gives a harsh quality to your great shouts of laughter, a scornful edge to them, and babies hearing this for the first time burst into tears.

You are clever at love, though rarely successful ('We don't set much store on *cleverness* at Albion House'). You have a libido the size of your liver, and both can be diseased (especially by alcohol). But it is not women you love, it is girls. Girls under 25, you can't have too many girls under 25 – girls in summer dresses, girls in ball gowns and bare shoulders, upper-class girls with lazy mouths and arrogant eyes, girls with light brown hair on their forearms, girls who laugh and squeal and squirm in their seats when you say things, girls who sit properly with a sway in their back, American girls with green eyes in the Crush Bar, girls in Scotch House sweaters, pretty girls in Eton collars, French girls in bikinis with a gold chain as thin as two interwoven hairs round one ankle. 'I must have them!' you think and sometimes say, 'or I shall *die*!' They rather like it when you say that. At least they like it more than when you say, 'My dear, how I long to see you in my Bentley with your skirt round your waist.' They squeal at that, and squirm, but you very rarely get to see them in the back of your Bentley.

You tease girls of this sort, and all sorts, and the sense of distant hostility in your eyes, as faint as a homeopathic aftertaste, is strangely exciting to certain of them. But exciting as it may be, it loses its effect as time goes by – you never open up to them as you led them to believe you would. However much you demand of them, you walk out, often rather grandly, when they demand anything of you. You told them sadly at the beginning of your affair, as long as ten days ago, that it would probably end like this and they found it rather attractive then, the sadness of life, autumn, fruit, Keats, Oxford, et in arcadia ego. They didn't realize it would all be over *quite* so quickly.

This is actually your best bargaining talent, setting up the initial contract. You never over-commit yourself, and some of the clauses in the fine print are drafted as well as any insurance shark could. You allow women to believe many things about your generosity that are not in the end true. You can be generous, but only if you get a good return. You do nothing for the simple pleasure of doing it.

You do not like flawed women, women with warts or webbed fingers. It has a morbid effect on your romantic life as your lovers must be perfect. When you find a perfect woman she turns out to be foreign, or her laugh's too loud, or she says stupid things. And even if she isn't, or doesn't, *and* she likes you, *and* the affair is consummated, it *still* only lasts ten days. You can have a pretty sparse love life, you Librans.

You never give all the heart, and only occasionally give any of the heart at all. But you do give a lot of advice, and this can look as though you are taking an interest. You rhyme your way into women's hearts, and reason your way out.

Sexually

Your sexual organ, you tell women in Perrier bars, weighs seven lbs. and is so big you can't get your fingers around it (you're talking about your brain) and this causes some disappointment later in the relationship.

You can be a little insubstantial in bed – you are not enmeshed in the material world as Earth signs are, you do not understand the flesh, what it is or what it's for. When it goes wrong, and you get fluid retention, or bad legs, you are aware of the flesh, but when you are trying to squeeze pleasure out of it, or mystery, you are seen at your most inept. You know where to put your hands (you've read the books), you may even know where to move them, but you don't know when. Your astonishing selfishness hinders satisfactory relations, too, and inhibits the harmony of movement between you; the assonance and consonance of good sex will be dulled and confused. You also suffer from premature ejaculation, alcoholic impotence and a penis the size of a cocktail sausage.

Mental Air signs bend to perversion, and your fertile mind can be highly perverted. A lot of it happens in your head, which is all very well for you but may be unsatisfactory for anyone else in the bed at the time. Your theatrical background encourages you to like tableaux vivants, when you can gorge at length on women. You browse over their round bodies as they gently stretch. You might like to get in among them, but only as an observer, unnoticed, to do what you wanted without them knowing, like a little boy, like a cherub.

You can't get close to anyone without wanting to get closer. You want to get inside every girl you know. All of you. Your whole body inside her, there's *something* going odd going on here, they think, as you try to do it.

Post-coitally you roll away into your own world, and lie there looking up into the dark at the back of your brain. When your appetites fail you can disappear, so this is a dangerous time for you. Your partner is being gentle and loving and caring, but wet with the sex-slick, and you're looking up into the dark for a faint star. No wonder your affairs are so rarely successful.

Most importantly, though – every time you sleep with a different girl, a light goes out.

Things Libran Men Say

Don't get too involved.

I need to keep my freedom.

I'm not ready for a commitment.

I told you when I came I was a stranger.

Things Librans Know

That risk and opportunity are the same words in Chinese.

Maritally

You are sensitive to noise, particularly to women's voices,

particularly to women's voices telling you to put the rubbish out. But luckily you are clever. You are very clever; in fact, you're so clever you're terribly unhappy. It's because you're so elusive. For someone who talks as much as you do it is incredible how quickly you can retreat into long, sulky silences (they can last up to a year – love means never being the first to say you're sorry). It can be frightening, like a fit, when you make your face go blank, suddenly there's a haemorrhage in the side of the room. This makes it difficult to get close to you. You are actually a very private person, though you can hide behind a transparent façade of complete frankness. When you've told everything about yourself they still are none the wiser. Perhaps this is why you never tell anyone you love them after you're married, not unless you want something very, very badly. You will adapt to suit your partner, but you will expect your partner to change for you too – you exact payment quite scrupulously, and if you aren't paid you come looking for revenge (see *Great Enragers*).

Great Enragers

Faced with overwhelming odds, the Libran may become curiously inert, like a rabbit petrified in headlights. You cannot win, but if you can't, you make sure she won't either, and eventually you may take up covert guerilla action to even the score. You are clever enough to store the knowledge of what really annoys your wife – the subtle mechanisms of disapproval, which words, which looks, which innocent questions ('Shall I carve now?') . . . it might be a certain waistcoat, a wrong tie, a particular pudding at a restaurant, and suddenly there is an incandescent woman and an innocent Libran coping magnificently. 'He's *marvellous* they way he puts up with her,' your friends say, and only the briefest look of gratitude plays on your face before you say 'Oh she's a great girl, I wouldn't have her any other way.'

The Importance Of Mutual Privacy

Though the sign is one of sharing and cooperation there are some things beyond intimacy, and your married life needs separate bathrooms. You can meet in the bedroom, but the most exciting thing that happens here is dressing for dinner with a pitcher of martinis. This appeals to your sense of tradition, and you act it out as they used to in the old films when you were a little boy: she has to tie your tie, which she does in three deft movements and pats your chest; you will kiss her nose; you both go downstairs and say goodnight to your attractive children, and leave them with your competent nanny, and go out to a musical comedy (you have a box) with your attractive friends.

You Are Not Good At Marriage

Amazingly, for a sign dedicated to marriage, harmony and mutual cooperation, you haven't got the stomach for marriage. Wives don't let you do absolutely everything you want to, and the sense of cooperation falls down. Neither can you take the bruises, or the broken heads, the drunken arguments at 3 a.m. You can't take the surprise attacks, the exposed flanks, the flak, the battery. Women, or at least wives, you conceive, are just too much of the material world. You marry more than once but it doesn't change anything.

You fight fiercely though, especially when winning. However, you don't like crushing victories either, so you're always picking your victim up and propping them up to keep their dignity intact. Though if they annoy you further you will crack them down again. Your hysterical sense of fair play is your most impenetrable defence.

Dealing With The Libran

He is incredibly demanding, he expects you to know what he is thinking (his quicksilver mind makes it impossible for him to explain the simplest operation, or to stick to the most elementary schedule). And he never knows what it is that's worrying him, and you certainly don't either, how could you, are you a mind reader? And because he's so stupid and cowardly, and doesn't know what he feels about anything, he doesn't get at you for something that's bugging him, he gets at you for something completely different about a *week* later, and there's a *filthy* row, and neither of you really know what about, and then he goes and sleeps on the sofa, and doesn't say *any*thing for about three days which is the only time you can get a word in edgeways, so it's an ill wind, isn't it?

Women

Libran women are, according to Saint Augustine, particularly feminine: small ankles, small brain, large bottom – that's what St Augustine said. He also noted how your slim, beautifully manicured fingers find a man's perineum at his moment of crisis, and how popular this made you through the Middle Ages (especially with St Augustine). You also enjoy masculine insights, and you can join in ridiculous discussions about money supply and Northern Ireland.

Despite this, and unlike the Libran man, you do have a latent understanding of sensuality. Under the right hands you can glow and change colour. You move lazily and softly, and occasionally release small samples of psychic musk from underneath your perfect breasts, and this is why men turn to you with that worried expression on their face.

Socially

Your greatest pleasure is as a student of human nature. You are intensely interested in all aspects of human relations, and the colour of their carpets, and how many abortions they've had. You are a dedicated gossip; vicious gossip doesn't offend you, though in your most generous mode you don't actively participate in it, but listen carefully.

You are often the most aggrieved member of the Zodiac – so aware of your own high talents that no amount of appreciation is really appreciative enough for you. You make enthusiastic paranoids, as you must if you are to worry for your reputation as you do. You carry grudges, remember slights, pay back snubs. You log your public appearances in your head, and regularly calculate your viewing figures to assess your popularity.

But you are seen in society, and you spend freely to maintain your beautiful profile, a patriotic consumer. This is why you like older men – not only are they more sophisticated, more understanding, they also have more money.

To keep them in the game you apply your make-up more and more generously over the years. You may not be able to find your face when you're 50. It is your Libran talent to overdo everything you do, so be careful.

Sexually

You make the mistake of saying the one thing which terrifies men. You get away with it because you have a lot of sex appeal, and many possible partners. However, when you say 'Talk to me', you go too far. The poor fool is concentrating so on his productivity, getting the moving parts moving in a culturally acceptable way, and you whisper 'Talk to me' in his ear. What on earth about? We know you are intensely argumentative Mental Air sign, but there is a time and place for everything. You must at least give clues as to what you want the conversation to consist of – a broad hint might be 'Do you love me?' or 'What do you want to do to me? Where do you want to do it? In which emotional mode do you want to do it?' Without these hints ninety per cent of men are lost. And so is their sexual presence.

Much of your sex drive will go into interior decoration.

Ruled by Venus, there will be a tension between the masculine and feminine in your nature, as we see in Martina Navratilova.

Deep Down

You have a lot of style, perhaps too much. And though your house is skilfully done – the carpets are 80/20 wool twist and you have a blonde pine desk, and a wok – you sense something, somewhere is not quite right with your life. At the edge of your eye, sometimes you glimpse the foolishness of your life. And though you blink and turn away at once, yet it happens often enough to remind you what all life will become, in some colourless place. It generates a sense of melancholy in you, over the years, and the more so the closer you come to it. It's what might possibly redeem you from a silly and unsatisfactory life – though what difference that makes to anything, nobody knows.

In The Late Twentieth Century

With your savage ambitions, your neurotic longing for fame, your unbalanced attitude to work, you make the best citizens of post-industrial Europe. Money comes to you (you will do anything to get it), and you do your post-industrial duty of *spending* it. Success is, however, more elusive, and many of you have to get by without fame or the recognition of Michael Parkinson. You never appreciate just how lucky you are in this.

Friends you grew up with will be annoyed at whatever you achieve – outside of a Pentonville sentence – as with some justification they assumed you would suffer some flame-out, you would auto-destruct, your mission would be aborted. Well, perhaps it will, but for now you do terribly, terribly well.

You are pleasant to be with socially, and maybe even personally (though less than your charming persona suggests). But publicly, your mad ambition deprives you of your full potential. A scent in your nostril leads you astray, a scent of glamour and success. It does to you what a drop of blood in a swimming pool does to a shark. It makes you mad. Remember, a momento mori, the remains of Clive James.

The Librans

Margaret Thatcher, Sir Robert Muldoon, Leon Brittan, Gerry Adams, Christopher Booker, Heinrich Himmler, Bruce Springsteen, the Duke of Fife, Mickey Rooney, Konstantin Chernenko, Sir Michael Edwardes, Ray Charles, Baroness Orczy, Linda McCartney, Anthony Newley, F. Scott Fitzgerald, Christopher Reeve, Felicity Kendall, Ian Chappell, Bryan Ferry, Sir Barnes Wallis, Michele Dotrice, Gordon Honeycombe, Alvin Stardust, Jeremy Isaacs, Sylvia Kristal, Marcello Mastroianni, Greer Garson, Richard Harris, Trevor Brooking, Don McLean, Jan Morris, Damon Runyon, Charlton Heston, Basil D'Oliveira, Buster Keaton, Sebastian de Ferranti, Glynis Johns, Robert Kee, Donald Pleasance, Clive James, Melvyn Bragg, Sir John Donaldson, Yaltah Menuhin, Jayne Torvill, Niels Bohr, Peter Wood, Donald Sinden, Bill Tidy, Alastair Sim, James Clavell, Fiona Fullerton, Helen Hayes, Daniel Massey, Nicholas Parsons, Harold Pinter, H.J. Heinz, A.P. Herbert, Ronnie Barker, Barbara Walters, T.S. Eliot, Olivia Newton John, George Gershwin, Bernard Miles, Brigitte Bardot, Sapper, Stevie Smith, Mrs Gaskell, Jack Wild, Rula Lenska, Angie Dickinson, Deborah Kerr, Truman Capote, Michael Innes, Donald Swan, Julie Andrews, Stanley Holloway, Sandy Gall, Jimmy Carter, Graham Greene, Anna Ford, Gandhi, Chubby Checker, Edith Cavell, Edwina Currie, Michael Heath, Sir Terence Conran, Barbara Kelly, Le Corbusier, Britt Ekland, Ray Reardon, Frank Herbert, Steve Ovett, Lord Hailsham, John Lennon, Martina Navratilova, Watteau, Eleanor Roosevelt, Aleister Crowley, Angela Rippon, Magnus Magnusson, Luciano Pavarotti, Lily Langtry, Dwight D. Eisenhower, Cliff Richard, Roger Moore, Mario Puzo, Lilian Gish, Oscar Wilde, P.G. Wodehouse, Max Bygraves, Peter Bowles, Angela Lansbury, the Earl of Cardigan, Elinor Glyn,

Rita Hayworth, Evel Knieval, Nietzsche, Simon Ward, Robert Stephenson, Margot Kidder, Kelly Monteith, Chuck Berry, Art Buchwald, Dame Anna Neagle, Dizzy Gillespie, Simon Gray, Leonard Rossiter, Sir Georg Solti, Lt. Col. John Blashford Snell, Pierre Trudeau, Melina Mercouri, Derek Jacobi, Jade Jagger, Sarah Bernhardt, John Le Carré, Lord Palmerston, S. T. Coleridge, Ursula le Guin, Alfred Nobel, Dory Previn, Joan Fontaine, Catherine Deneuve, Franz Liszt and Yo Yo Ma, the celebrated cellist.

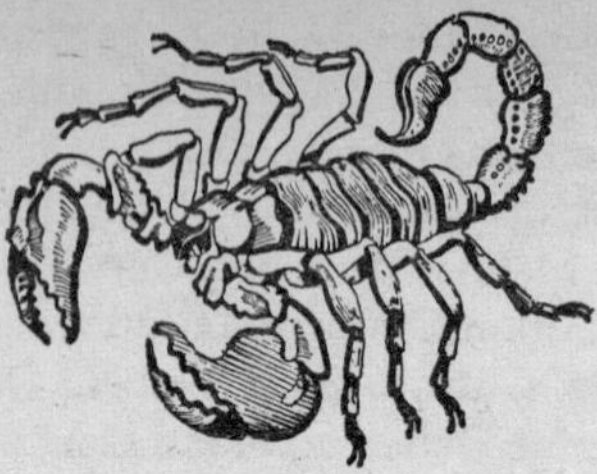

SCORPIO

24 October – 22 November

The Glyph

The sign is represented by the incompetent claws and ferocious stare of a malevolent arachnid. Both Evelyn Waugh and his son Auberon are Scorpios – no grappling intellect, but one perfect punch. Characteristically, both attack from an unexpected angle, up over their back in a scorpion strike.

Be careful, Scorpio – if your spine is too short the sting lands in the back of your head, and this can be fatal (Nigel Dempster is a Scorpio).

The Ruling Planet

Pluto rules Scorpio, and is responsible for much of your peculiarity. Pluto is the last planet in the solar system, far out in the gravity fields, small and cold, smaller and colder and further away even than New Zealand. The sun which gives so much light and heat to earth appears tiny and faint to Pluto, appears a distant star, nothing more than a navigation aid, very much as London appears from Auckland Harbour. Pluto is the last post before the great emptiness, the unimaginable distance, the invisible trillions of the emptying universe.

Astrologically Pluto stands as the great evacuant: it is death, degeneration, divorce, rebirth, it is wholesale destruction and new life. Pluto is getting the builders in. It is the unknown. It is whole new wardrobes of clothes. It is emptiness and darkness, mystery and magic.

Pluto means mass thinking, mass movements, great migrations, international currency surges. Knowledge of Pluto offers knowledge of the deep structure, the key to deep secrets, to the underworld, the negotiable bond market; Pluto points the way to the inner springs of the mystery, to nuclear power, the footwork of the radiation dance. This is the planet that rules your sign. It isn't uninteresting.

The Karma

The sign is Water, is fixed, is feminine, is negative. There must have been waste in your past lives, facetiousness, trivia, gaiety. Your current incarnation is dedicated to the development of your fighting tentacles, and the knowledge of power which that produces.

In your search for power, for that one frightening, overwhelming secret, you make charts of the outside world. But you are the fastest in the Zodiac to see that the maps that you make of the heavens or of the sub-atomic world are all maps of your own internal structure. All knowledge, you perceive, is knowledge of self. If you know everything about yourself you can deduce everything else.

This is why you go down into the maze of yourself: you are looking for the Minotaur.

Thus, to learn that Ken Dodd and Lulu are Scorpios makes them more interesting than they might have been. It is a shame that nothing on earth could make Scorpio Shaw Taylor interesting at all.

But It's Not All Good News

It must be said, though, that the Scorpio search for power often misfires – more misfits and derelicts, more street maniacs who develop psychological fighting systems akin to kung fu are Scorpios, more so than any other sign. But then more Scorpios are presidents of the United States, and indeed so is our own Prince Charles (but then – homeopathy, spiritualism, omelettes for dinner – he's getting rather odd these days too).

The Personality

You may not have much personality, but what you have is extremely strong. Your ego is as big as a Buick, and twice as unreliable (the clutch is always going, it engages the engine at the wrong time – the cause of many of your frustrations – or it doesn't engage at all: the motor races and nothing happens till it all blows up, very Scorpio).

On the good side, Dick Cavett and Johnny Carson are Scorpios, but on the downside so is Frank Delaney. Scorpio Anni-Frid was a member of Abba, though owing to Scorpio's obsessive secrecy critics are still unable to say exactly which member she was.

Rather than say what you think, Scorpios say nothing at all and this is just as well or you wouldn't have any friends. Small talk doesn't interest you (you're single biggest failing), but blood does, and disgust, and guts in a bucket (the sign is full of doctors. And indeed the Kray twins. And Michael Winner). There is little that is playful about you, little that is thoughtlessly generous. You give nothing away. Your blank face and level stare are designed to protect you from the world: you even wear sunglasses to conceal your inscrutability.

You make talented paranoids, you feel *something* is going on (as indeed it is) but what it is you don't yet know (you never will). Your strongest talent is self-control, and considering what you have to control in there, this is just as well. However, in your nova phase (when you explode) you attract much admiring commentary (Dylan Thomas, Charles Manson), though to everyone's relief you burn yourself out in the end. Self-control is vital to the Scorpio's continued interest in life: any loss of dignity in this increasingly respectable world and you find it hard to survive. Your animal instincts are powerful, and unfashionable. There is much unreconstructed appetite down there: Tiberius in his party mode exemplified, if not the best of Scorpio, then certainly the most.

Highly Charged Personality

The fact is that Scorpios are the least generally liked sign of the Zodiac. Your deep feelings are painful to those around you, but it doesn't stop you sharing them. Your magnetism is, by definition, attractive, but it is unlikeable. Your mean, mad, savage look gives you the appearance of the most sinister sort of Latin master, with your penetrating stare, your weakness for whisky and the long ferrules. Those closest to you don't enjoy dates with you; in spite of your self-control you are the wild card, the random factor, you are always on the edge of an altercation: dinner for two may end up in a lawsuit, a traffic fight, a police cell. As a paranoid you understand paranoia, and you can make it work for you – the level of anxiety rises in the room as you enter, and this makes party people perform. You are socially useful even though you have nothing social to say.

Lethal Companions

There is, in the Scorpio-born, a sense of something loping across the backblocks at a steady twenty k.p.h., eating everything it sees – weaklings, submissives, the sick. Scorpios have no general relationship with other people beyond the relationship a person has with a pork chop.

Expressed in your normal, everyday life, it is simply a great sense of competition. This can drive you into the highest levels of success, but you know you can easily degenerate as well, and frighteningly quickly too (have you seen David Hemmings recently? Or poor old Dickie Henderson?). You are inspired by opposition. Your nature is activated by contest, you will do anything to win (the things Australian wicket keeper Rodney Marsh says to distract Sri Lankan batsmen cannot be printed in any language).

It is not that you enjoy winning, it's that you enjoy beating people. This is why the humiliation of your opponent is more important than the fruits of freedom and victory – you win, but you stay to kick the corpse, to savage the body. In spite of your deeply mystical nature, you will never get to heaven. You are finally enmeshed in the flesh. You tell yourself you have the capacity to soar with the eagles, but your hunger for the jugular keeps you down in the welter of pain and darkness. The last public hanging in 1783 and the first issue of *Private Eye* were both Scorpio events.

The One Game You Lose

This is why death interests you. Because you have to win to live you find death the most compelling fact in life (many Scorpios are doctors, and if desperate, they become surgeons, so deeply afraid of dying they spend their lives inuring themselves to the horror of it). Part of your power with others derives from this, because you can stare unblinking at that which others cannot countenance. So you can look down into the abyss of yourself (only you have the fortitude to face what is there) because you feel that everything you need to know is inside – all filth and religion, cruelty and kinship, hatred and horror, Francis Bacon and Bill Wyman, Peter Cook and Sir Dudley Smith, the legion of Scorpio. You live dangerously, for when you look into the abyss, the abyss – sooner or later – looks back.

Surprisingly Bad At Fascism

When you Scorpios successfully assemble your personalities

you are quite without interest in the opinions of other individuals, or even in the individuals themselves (Martin Luther, Sir Sacheverell Sitwell). At a very slight turn of your head, whole classes of society disappear. You tend to use your colleagues, friends, marital associates as instruments of self-discovery. This is not an attractive habit, but at least you are individual. You also have individual ideas (so individual they are often unintelligible). You recoil from the vulgarity of public opinions and conventional wisdom – you will not say what you do not think, even after dinner, even for the sake of your hostess. Thus you do not get on well in a totalitarian society – despite your autocratic nature your sympathies are not actually with the Nazis, their vulgarity is too much for you, hugger-mugger with the lower classes. You have a patrician, but misanthropic nature. You exist in a world of your own, so much so that you often step into oncoming traffic.

But When You Go The Wrong Way

On those occasions when you Scorpios fail to assemble your personality according to instructions, then you suffer from severe disorders – psychological, social, psychosomatic. The Zodiac's best (Librans) may lack all conviction, but the worst (unreconstructed Scorpios) are filled with a passionate intensity. Things fall apart, the centre cannot hold, the Scorpions are loosed upon the world.

Unsuccessful Scorpions succumb to your biology – you become the instrument of your appetites – you long for money, success, drugs and fame, and you will do *any*thing, *any*thing to get what you want. And there you will be when the going gets tough – Joe Kennedy, Bob Haldeman, Will Rogers, and of course General Montgomery (though when the going gets too tough you shoot yourselves, as Goebbels did, rather than accept a judicial rebuke – Nuremburg in his case – as no Scorpio can accept criticism indifferently).

As an object you are immoveable, as a force irresistible, as a Scorpio hungry for admiration you exercise your dark talents.

In the descending spiral of your social ambitions you stir up hornets to help you. You hurt people to see how they will express pain – it's the most reliable method you know of seeing spontaneous behaviour (so controlled are you yourself that you are suspicious of everyone else). This tendency may provoke a hostile defence from a victim, but your counterstrike is annihilating, to 'kill not only him, but all his family and friends, and burn down his house and sing comic songs in the ruins'. No one is less forgiving than you, particularly in the smaller matters – you find it easier to forgive your wife's divorce action than being flicked on the nose by a police interrogator (it may take ten years but sooner or later that young constable will find his cat crucified, his children missing, his fridge full of poisoned horse manure).

Your Friends Are Wary

Though you are known to be loyal to your friends, astrologers are beginning to wonder whether this reputation is just a propaganda victory for the sign. The fact is that the administration of paranoia is your single most effective social strategy. You unsettle opponents (everyone who does not agree with you in tones of manic affirmation is an opponent) by remarks such as 'You're not a well-liked person, you know,' and this creates doubt in an efficient, effective manner. 'You say you have friends, and it may be true, but *nobody likes them*!' You say things no civilized person would say, in a very urbane way: 'Everyone I know has said how silly it looks when the tip of your nose moves when you laugh.' Or again, 'The cat you gave Valerie has been found again, after you lost it, but it was found *dead*, and the police say it *had been tortured to death*.' You like that a great deal, especially when it isn't true. You get under the skin, you come in from an unexpected angle, behind the defence, and lay about yourself, mopping up the pawn structure while your friends scurry worriedly around their defensive ranks. This is an individual interpretation of the concept of loyalty, but then as we've noted, you are individual beyond understanding.

Other Talents

All you Scorpios believe yourselves to be talented (especially when you're not), but the intensity you bring to your belief can startle others into believing it too. You can get away with it for years; the process of reputation is self-regenerating, as long as you tend it. One of your primary qualities, apart from *wicked* ambition, is watchfulness, perpetual alertness, vigilance; you make gossip columnists, social commentators, hit and run journalists, blackmailers, conspirators, terrorists, madmen and bad artists. You know about human nature (and you don't care much for it); you are not sensitive but you can register what others are feeling, and you do not make allowances for failure. Scorn is your most frequent reaction, though you can occasionally be amused – the one perfect punch in your personality is rarely left unused: knowledge is the ammunition in your arsenal, and you have a passion to know. There is a coldness about you, a clear sightedness, and you can be allergic to alcohol for this reason. This helps your career a good deal, and your diaries. Your database is very detailed, it's what counts as knowledge: knowledge is power, and your files and diaries are very explicit, you forget nothing and you never forgive.

The Scorpio Child

The early socialization of Scorpios is therefore a major task and may require much parental violence. It is easy to sense the intensity of the Scorpio baby, and the parents are the first to feel fear. They wonder whether their real baby was swapped at the hospital, or whether your mother had inadvertent relations with the Devil. No one enjoys the process of breaking you in, least of all yourself. Sometimes, with enough skilful whipping it turns out well (Prince Charles), and sometimes we are unlucky if it turns out at all (Ian *Sproat*).

The formative years, consequently, cast a longer shadow over the Scorpio's development than other, more carefree signs. The mystery of life that Scorpio senses probably starts here – how can these great, slothful apes with their huge bodies and low I.Q.s have all this authority? You will never put up with it again.

Romantically

You have a way with the opposite sex, and it is generally your own way.

Love is the most profoundly political event in your experience. Your seductions are powerplays, there is rarely a great sense of common interest and shared enjoyment, except when you are young and don't know any better.

Other signs should not be taken in by apparent generosity. You will be revealing aspects of yourself as part of a bargain, the terms of which have yet to be driven ('I've invited you to my home, I've introduced you to my parents. . .'): the apparently casual invitation will be regenerated as a cross between a court presentation and an engagement party. If you are the Minotaur it's astonishing that anyone dare enter the maze.

So Why Do They Put Up With You?

You have the personality that inspires the most extreme dislike – and this is the first stage of the most successful and spectacular seductions.

Your quiet strength may also be admired, and the sense of danger underneath your artificially calm exterior is compelling to many women. You have the glamour of a person with many friends (like all glamour it is more style than substance); you offer knowledge, contact with the world, passion, ignition, lift-off. By the time they discover the terms of trade it is too late

– they're already sitting face in hands at the kitchen table, tears blotching up their complexion.

Women can look at Scorpio men with amusement (bad actors in a bad book of passion), but when Scorpio men look back, the same women may be startled out of their clothes. Just like that.

And You Can Be Irresistible

Even though you have no sense of humour you can be irresistible. You are at your most irresistible when employing classic interrogation techniques to win your way (tough-cop, nice-cop, an alternation of sympathy and savagery). You shift the ground from under the opposition's feet – they find themselves giddy with bewilderment, utterly destabilized – they cling on to the only fixed point in the exploding world, the most solid thing to hand is often your priapic asset, no wonder you succeed so easily.

Terrorist Sex Life

You approach through the undergrowth at the back of the house, and enter before she knows you're there. Once in you stay in. It takes tear-gas and stun-grenades to get you out. You may deceive your partner, but only to examine her credulity – you will not feel that your integrity has been impaired. Thus you may offer the information that you sleep with a waitress on Wednesdays/you are involved in a homosexual marriage/you are going to kill her now – but not out of malice, just to surprise her into giving something away.

But withdrawing from a relationship is not easy. Your bonding chemicals are powerful, and divorce is a very mixed blessing to the Scorpio (like losing a leg).

But So Self-Contained

It is fortunate for the institution of marriage that you Scorpio men are so reserved, because the fact is that although many try to resist you, you can have any woman you want. And many men that you don't. You charge the atmosphere with a sexual current, and this, like drugs, allows women to abandon their inhibitions.

You also know her pressure points and can play them like a pianist. You have the gift of certainty – you appear to be utterly without doubt and this affects many women. They don't necessarily like it but it is effective, because this, too, offers defined space in which anything is allowed to happen. She has a great sense of privacy, covered in the secret den of your personality.

To Seduce A Male Scorpio

Scorpio men are aroused by a glimpse of weakness, a moment of indecision; Scorpio's priapic behaviour is aroused by an opening for his talent. To seduce a Scorpio, stand with your hand momentarily at your mouth, and puzzlement playing on your best feature (not your breasts).

The Scorpio will be on you, as quick as a crocodile, the Scorpio will be on you to make you his creature – so use the technique sparingly.

Sexually, Male

You Scorpios are solidly put together, you are sexually effective – carnivorous, dark, and rather unattractive, like Welshmen. However, you take sex seriously, and intensely, though the intensity is rarely allowed out, kennelled in a private hell, feeding on itself. As you grow older you realize how powerful an engine it can be, what a force all the hatred and hunger, the scorn and the anger can be, and the appetite – in its fullest expression it makes unusual and unattractive sexual relations but – and this is most important – at least you are never sexually *vulgar*. Casual sex is impossible for you, as for your partner (you'd kill them). Neither are you interested in display (the opinions, the admiration of any individual is unimportant to you) and films, fetishes, special clothing, technical apparatus offer no excitement in themselves (though you may experiment with any combination to see appetite ignite in your partner's eye).

But when you go the wrong way no perversion is too disgusting for you (see *Women*).

A Serious Sexual Being

You feel that the sexual act reaches down into the springs of life itself, and that information about society, about the universe, about death is released as a by-product of industrious sexual activity.

Thus you are aware that this is the only way women may reveal their complete nakedness – layers rolling off themselves as something utterly untouched emerges – but your women should realize that *you are not interested in the revelation*! It is the by-product you value, it is knowledge of death and the dance of radiation, the knowledge of mass movements you deduce from personal movements; the spheres of life that Pluto represents make you shake with excitement. It is life and death down there, all happening at once, where mind and matter intersect, a blend of mind and body, a pulse of blood, a flux of flow, in this Scorpion sexual waste disposal unit.

It can be awkward because women may feel, not unreasonably, that it is them you actually like and not all this other sort of thing.

Frightful Primitive

Perhaps this is the mystery in the flesh that keeps you alive. *'Where is it? Where is it?'* you hiss in your sleep. And you grip women, grip the flesh of them, squeezing it, biting it, sucking at it to process their mystery into your mind, magimixing it.

Scorpio men in touch with ancient, cruel religions eat the hearts of their enemies to make themselves strong.

Their enemies are women.

The Chickens

What is it about your touch that penetrates so deeply?

When farmers pick up a chicken in the yard, the chicken will struggle in his hand – unless the farmer intends to kill it. In that case the bird, somehow identifying the farmer's intention (How? By some darkness in his mind? Some awful colour in his aura?) just relaxes, goes wholly limp, resigns itself, surrenders, composes itself for death.

Women are like that when you Scorpio men really want to go to bed with them. You touch them and they go limp, even if they want to resist they don't. They see some awful colour in your aura, and they surrender.

Actually Doing It

So it is, you Scorpio men are able to go to bed with any woman you genuinely (though not desperately) want to. The vigour of your admiration sears women like a solar flare, a flash of highly energized plasma which hits her from all sides at once.

When your hands slide inside her sweater her eyelids flutter and her flesh creeps. You inspire horror and desire equally, even as you struggle with the continental popper system of her brassiere. You are the only sign of the Zodiac that can get out of trousers gracefully. The sexual flush you generate on her mouth, cheeks and chest is so hot that she finds herself on the wrong side of her underwear without any knowledge of how it happened.

She thought it was dinner for two and an early night (she's flying to Cannes on the early flight tomorrow). But here she is, she doesn't know how, it's like a psychedelic drug experience: it's 2 a.m., on the floor of her hall with her legs in the air, her panties are still on, but pushed aside, her mouth registering shock (and possibly horror) but there is a gathering sense somewhere in the pit of her body of a genital bomb releasing radiation to ever-increasing levels of danger. For the only moment in her married life that she can ever remember, she is not aware of her children. The layers are rolling back for the emergence of her new virginity.

You may not be liked but, as they say of Lulu's singing voice, you are certainly effective.

A Scorpio Deformity

When women climax in the company of a Scorpio they may hang on to your ears to keep themselves in this world – and it hurts. This may explain the shape of Scorpio Prince Charles' abnormal aural organs.

Your Weak Points

Apart from your sense of humour, your weak points may be your back and your sexual organs – which, considering the use to which you put them, is not surprising.

Maritally

The power broking interests you in the initial stages, and the fight for the matrimonial territory too, but once the terms of the treaty have been established, once the level of reparations has been struck, the POWs released and the war criminals hanged, then married life ceases to be the source of your most intense life.

The casual violence of your successful marriages may appal everyone else, and terrify your children: attacks on your spouse they construe as attacks on themselves. This is why the little things sit at the top of the stairs rocking with horror when they hear you fighting through the night.

You may find surprises help you to maintain interest – letters from your wife's counsel are particularly effective.

Women

The healthy Scorpio woman is one of the most intensely alive women in the Zodiac. She is brought into being as a focus of her desires – these operate like lenses, like radio telescopes beaming information into a central matrix. A perfect blend of appetite and desire, love and sex, mind and body, gin and tonic. She takes only what she can give. There are nine healthy Scorpio women in the UK.

You are less equipped for conventional happiness than any woman in the Zodiac. You are a demanding woman, and happiness is not one of the things you demand. Knowledge is what you want, you think it will make you safe. It won't, as it happens, but anyway you want it; you chart all the cracks and traps of your personality, and of others, for knowledge is power, and you believe power will give you strength. But you have seen, haven't you, really powerful men, men who can administer a constricting budget, and you know how contemptibly weak they are when you play with their switches. You have seen, as few other signs see, lust in action. Or if not lust, then appetite, and perverted appetite at that.

Also, men sense that your hunger for knowledge is greater than good sense normally allows, and they encourage you to reach inside them for the unspeakable, the inexpressible, the unaccountable. They want you to dress them in knee breeches and humiliate them with a wooden spoon; they want to wear your underwear and preen themselves in windows; they want to be tied to a bondage bar and penetrated with root-crop vegetables, they want to watch it in slow-motion on the video. And you will collaborate in all this, not for pleasure, or profit, or even to find out about yourself, but solely in order to be able to despise them later, to exercise your scorn on them, to control them, rise above the dross of them afterwards. It helps your career too – as Scorpio-born Vivien Leigh in Hollywood found to her cost.

But Tricky With It

Sometimes you can go into a submissive posture, as a lure for the over-eager – they rear up in front of you, exposing themselves to your annihilating counter-strike.

These things you do just to see what happens, and you think you won't be marked by the experience. To an extent you are right: more than other signs you can pass through degrading and humiliating experiences without being degraded or humiliated (Petula Clarke's singing career is a fine Scorpion example), but the complexity of sex, the trade of information and desire, the urgent, penetrating demands – you have so many balls to keep in the air, it's harder than you think to control everything at once, and you may well find yourself stretched further than you can take – you may find yourself caught up in it, you may find yourself taking the ridiculous aspects of perverted relations seriously.

As a case in point – you attract masochists, and as you experiment on them you are drawn into their net. The sadist is in a weaker position than the masochist: the former needs the latter more than vice versa. This can have a morbid effect on your sexual profitability.

A Goer, Though, A Self-Starter

Boys trawl alongside you on summer evenings and try to get you into the car. They say things like, 'Let's drive to Land's End!' You get into the car, and this makes them shift in their seat. They sense you are a sexual welterweight, that you will require multiple orgasms, and this alarms small groups who fear they will not be adequate to your needs (they won't).

Your sense of adventure generally takes things from bad to worse. You don't flirt with men, you drive on single-mindedly into the stockyards, to get busy. You are statistically more involved in rape attacks, on either side, slightly less often as the victim.

Something in your astrology inspires you to a wild over-reaction to men, sex, marriage, drugs, and for this reason you can be lonely in later life (i.e. your thirties – it all happens early for the Scorpio, it's all over before you had a chance to get going).

Premature burn-out is therefore a problem for many of you – you've used up all your appetites before you can properly enjoy them, and early middle age can find you empty and vaguely discontented, like the victim of experimental brain surgery. It may simply be that you drink too much. Or not drink enough: the furious alcoholic dislocations can be helpful, especially when there is nothing else in your life. But you knew it was possible to squander emotional capital if for no other reason than your mother used to tell you. You never believed her, and you were wrong.

Sexually

You don't need love before sex. You have a five-litre sex drive; you need a lot of it just for nourishment, it's food and drink for you, and you often want to make a pig of yourself. You operate best in competitive sex – you generally know better than anyone else in the bed, and you end up on top directing the sexual traffic.

You want to wallow in a trench of sex, you want to drown in flesh. Down in the chamber of passion all hell is breaking loose – wiring shorts, feedback building, delivery units overloading thermostats and rheostats glowing in the dark, and a terrible energy flashing through the brainblood and the neuro-circuitry; alarm horns are firing everywhere as the pressure builds in spasms, this is the life. Your sex grips him like a fist, and when you flex your strength down there it may make him nervous, he may be watching you carefully.

In the act of sex you give off an energy unknown to medical science; by a cabbalistic trick you let out a swathe of sexual ectoplasm which wraps around your partner like a stunning visual effect.

You may be a slow starter, and should avoid Gemini lovers (whose genital activities last about as long as a stop-light).

The guilt you feel at the end of your affairs (particularly the piggier) is not surprising, but neither is it helpful: it never stops you doing it again, and perhaps this is just as well.

Maritally

Stubborn, arrogant, domineering, overbearing you may be, but you very rarely wish your partner's death, either physical or psychic. You may reduce him to exhaustion but never to an object – you kick him back to consciousness again, breaking parts of him perhaps, you don't care, his weakness doesn't interest you.

You can be successful in the killing fields of matrimony. Though death horrifies you it doesn't frighten you, and you may often be able to prise loose your husband's grip on death (you feel men seek death in routine and in fantasy, in set figures they can control – you want energy from them, spontaneity, living savagery) and this may use up the years in a satisfying manner. At least you will be unlikely to wonder where it all went when you're 50. Even though you burned out and now have a quiet life you will look back and know the years you had. You won't still feel just 18 years old, still just on the brink of life, with everything just about to happen . . .

Career

Though you are an accomplished and independent businesswoman (your skill with money can be prodigious), you have a fatal flaw in your commercial make-up which is sexual in origin. During intense sexual experiences your breath comes in rasps and your eyes roll back in your head like grapes on a pin. This alarms business associates, for, owing to your confusion of money and sex you will terrify the client even as his pen is poised over the lease-deal.

Like few others in the Zodiac, the world exists supremely in your head. When you're wrong, everyone's wrong. When you close your eyes, it's night. Housemasters and divisional managers complain about your lack of team spirit (but only behind your back).

The Scorpios

Robin Day, the Kray Twins, Auberon Waugh, Evelyn Waugh, the first hydrogen bomb test, John Wells (oh ha ha), Peter Cook, W.S. Gilbert, Tiberius, Quentin Crewe, Indira Ghandi, Burt Lancaster, Juliet Mills, Daniel Boone, Conor Cruise O'Brien, Ludovic Kennedy, Loretta Swit, Lena Zavaroni, General Sir John Hackett, P.J. Proby, Christian Barnard, Iain *Sproat*, Karen Dotrice, Donald Trelford, Richard Burton, Martin Luther, Alger Hiss, Rodney Marsh, June Whitfield, Anni-Frid, Willie Carson, Field Marshal Montgomery, David Hemmings, Kim Wilde, Paul Foot and eco-brother of James, Teddy Goldsmith, Ronald Harwood, and Harold Larwood, Tim Rice, Bill Wyman, Dick Cavett, Fred Housego, Pablo Picasso, Lord Macaulay, Johann Strauss the Younger, Mahalia Jackson, Jodie Foster, Marie Antoinette, Edwin Hubble, Alastair Cook, Beryl Bainbridge, Johnny Mercer, Viscount Massereene and Ferrard, Pele, Baroness Young, the Hungarian Uprising, Phil Bennet, awful old Frank Delaney, Shaw Taylor, Anton van Leeuwenhoek, Dame Sybil Thorndike, Helen Reddy, François Mitterand, Bob Hoskins, Bob Haldeman, Lord Moyne, Monica Sims, Chris Tavare, Paganini, the Shah of Iran, Hugh Scanlon, Dylan Thomas, John Cleese, Sheridan, Eddie Charlton, Charles Moore, Harry Oppenheimer, David Dimbleby, Cleo Laine,

John Keats, Ezra Pound, Dick Francis, L.S. Lowry, Gary Player, Sir John Sainsbury, Viscount Linley, Ludovic Kennedy, Francis Bacon, Goebbels, Dickie Henderson, Henry Winkler, Michael Winner, Hogarth, Katherine Hepburn, Larry Holmes, Charles Bronson, Lulu, Walter Cronkite, Will Rogers, Tatum O'Neal, Vivien Leigh, Lester Piggot, John Philip Souza, Mike Nichols, Jean Shrimpton, Nigel Havers, Joan Sutherland, Marie Curie, Joni Mitchell, Albert Camus, Bram Stoker, Ken Dodd, King Edward VII, Carl Sagan, Richard Burton, Elizabeth Cadell, Roy Jenkins, Lucky Luciano, Princess Grace of Monaco, Charles Manson, Robert Louis Stevenson, Prince Charles, Claude Monet, August Rodin, Richmal Crompton, Peter Phillips, Petula Clarke, Daniel Barenboim, Sir Oswald Mosley, Griff Rhys Jones, Peggy Fenner, Ron Greenwood, Fenella Fielding, the Boulting Brothers, Sir Yue-Kong Pao, and Tina Brown.

SAGITTARIUS

23 November – 21 December

The Glyph

Half human, half horse; half man, half beast, like the editors of the *News Of The World*.

Having the centaur's tall perspective you stand out effortlessly in a crowd. You cruise around town freely and often in four-wheel drive, all-terrain vehicles, *which doesn't embarrass you*. By an astrological anomaly the sign includes no member of the Royal Family (except Caroline Kennedy).

Like classic Sagittarians William Blake and Alexander Solzhenitsyn, you combine the high idealism of evolved man (the archer aims at high spiritual targets) with the largest sexual apparatus of any in the zodiac.

For modern Sagittarians this is expressed by Woody Allen, sitting on Dick van Dyke's shoulders.

The Karma

You incorporate the duality of man and animal, reason and flesh, beauty and beast, love and sex. Life is a dialogue between your head and your hindquarters. Like Noel Coward. Though the hindquarters in his case generally belonged to someone else. It is this tension that pushes you into your search for deep truth. You can see further and move faster than any other sign and this offers scope for great improvement. You turn knowledge into wisdom with great appetite, absorbing the data, digesting the evidence, depositing the wisdom wherever you feel the need. But all too often you spoil the effect when you drop your trousers, release a tremendous barking fart and glare around you: *'Who did that!'* Winston Churchill did it. Bette Midler tries not to do it. Frank Zappa doesn't even try.

This extraordinary mix of high purpose and low behaviour is entirely typical of Sagittarians. Sloane men are statistically over-represented in this sign. As is Pamela Stephenson. At your noblest you glow with the spirit of religion, though you have no understanding of dogma, no patience with the bureaucracy, no sympathy with the large collection of plate. You find sermons in stones, and prayers in pasture; in your role as muscular Christian you place your outfield according to the Stations of the Cross.

But despite your tremendous spiritual energy, you may find that you lack direction. The deep restlessness in your soul offers you an affinity with desperados: you dream of freedom, of riding fences on the high plains. But beware this lack of Saturnine discipline as you may wake up, aged 50, all over the place, like a madwoman's breakfast. Or like Pat Phoenix. It's only too easy for a Sagittarian woman at a certain age.

It is the work of your incarnation in this tenth sign of the Zodiac (it's later than you think) to learn steadiness, subtlety, modesty, high resolution and carefulness. But don't go overboard or you'll end up like Sagittarian Cliff Michelmore. Read your old school reports for your karmic briefing.

Your Ruling Planet, Jupiter

This planetary influence offers great expansion, generosity, and tolerance of a wide range of social behaviour (which, considering the way Sagittarians behave, is important). It is the planet of wild exaggeration. Traditionally Jupiter offers high employment, successful pay claims and equal opportunity (for those with the right attitude). It promises optimism, rising scales, major chords, the great successes, if there were any successes, of triumphant liberalism. The planet encourages individual endeavour, demand-side economics, major public works, full employment, inflating currencies, greater trade, greater confidence, greater self-importance, and a greater desire to invade the Falklands.

Major Personality Traits

You have a major personality and all its traits are major, like hawsers. There is little that is subtle, or meticulous, or intricate about you. Ian Botham's behaviour is classic Sagittarian, as is the voice of *News Of The World* ex-editor Derek Jameson ('To ignore Jameson's accent would be to ignore a man at a party wearing a false nose'). John Osborne's plays are not strictly Sagittarian, however, being more the result of general indigestion than spontaneous combustion – an important element in this sign's temper is a cheerful lack of malice.

This is a big, bounding, boisterous sign, the sign of getting drunk and behaving boldly in restaurants. Honest without being virtuous, energetic without being deliberately rude, so straightforward many of you are actually on PAYE, Sagittarians make popular prefects until well into your forties. Eammon Andrews is a rare exception to this, along with Gordon Jackson, Oliver Cromwell, Kerry Packer and the Piltdown Man – the only unpopular Sagittarians in the Zodiac. You are what the advertising industry calls pro-active (the opposite of re-active – you don't simply act, and certainly don't need to react as you're too far ahead), and you express yourself in the imperative Square Mile Speech that is native to office-block Manhattan ('*Win* that contract!' '*Write* that book!' '*Challenge* that tax assessment!' '*Wipe* that smirk off your face!').

As a Sagittarian you behave badly, and travel. Often the two are linked, never more spectacularly than in the case of Lord 'Lucky' Lucan.

There has been a vogue for playing God as a Sagittarian over the last ten years – pleasant, benevolent, powerful, absent-minded. Ralph Richardson is cast as this, and rightly so, for he was born under this sign as perhaps no other was.

The Sagittarian's Spiritual Home

Despite Ralph Richardson, it must be said that England – so reserved, romantic, so intricate, seeking some mysterious balance between private urges and public requirements – is not a Sagittarian nation. The foremost Sagittarian nation is America with its loud voice and huge appetite. It stands out boldly in the world, is famous for its cheerful clumsiness, kind heart, fat wallet; it is frequently capable of the worst behaviour for the best reasons, is given to adventuring round the world in the oldest tradition of liberal imperialism, with aid, comfort, rocket attacks and Coca Cola. It has more energy than any other country in the world, but then it uses more. It eats Mars Bars not by nibbling off the perimeter chocolate, stripping off the caramel and licking the whipped centre section; America just bites off the end and gobbles at it. This is what they call foreign policy.

Highly Energetic

Ideas come to you with such force that you have to express them at once ('I have a terrible sinus pain.' 'Have them *drained*.') and this can get you a reputation for thoughtlessness. Your natural thoughtlessness augments this reputation. ('I don't need to tell you after all your miscarriages, do I?'). What is on the lung is on the tongue, as you like to say. The beefy cheerfulness you do so well is particularly offensive: 'Didn't think your *book* was very good old boy,' or alternatively, 'Thought your *book* was awfully good – who designed the cover?' You are simply unaware of the effect of your words – not that you don't care, you just don't know, no matter how you try: 'All those with mothers take one pace forward *Harrington where d'you think you're going!*'

This over-developed need for expression gives you a reputation for being outstandingly honest – though, like Aquarians, you are better at being candid than honest, as you are generally in too much of a hurry to develop genuine integrity. Tact is not in your armoury of social talents. 'I'd hurry up and get married if I were you, can't you find a man? Is that the problem? But if you don't have a baby soon you won't be able to have one at all, unless it's a mongol, I'm warning you.' The real object in all this is to preserve your position in the centre of the conversation. This is where you are most fully alive, with everyone looking at you. You don't mind whether people love you or hate you as long as they notice you. Your deepest need, underlying all others, even in this relatively evolved sign of the Zodiac, is to keep the most amount of attention focused on you for the most amount of time. This makes you attractive both to the Metropolitan Police, and a particular sort of savage woman (a profoundly unsettling idea for Sagittarian Robert Robinson, lest she disturb the foot of hair which is combed across his head and stuck down with invisible gel).

Gotta Dance

The high idealism that keeps you in the centre of the world also keeps you slightly above it, looking down over the fields, rivers, cities of your influence. When you say 'Put your left foot in', *millions* may do the Hokey Cokey. Your major personality addresses a crowd as easily as a one or two – more easily in fact: the larger the audience the less chance of backchat.

Your need for the spotlight draws you to unpopular causes, smaller businesses, freelance activity – you would much rather be the star of a small opposition than a henpecked minister in the government.

The perfect expression of the older, and successful Sagittarian personality is Henry Root:

> Dear Major-General Wyldbore Smith,
>
> I'm a blunt man accustomed to plain speaking so I'll come straight to the point. What's the going price for getting an honour?
>
> I do not mean a CBE or an OBE, which seem to be reserved for crooners, or those who are quick over the high hurdles. I see you have an OBE yourself. Nothing wrong with that! Well done!
>
> I enclose a pound. This is for yourself personally, you understand, and there's plenty more where that came from.

Note the bounding good humour, the vaulting ambition, the abrasive intimacy, the great beefy solidity of the prose style, the like of which hasn't been seen since Dornford Yates. However, when Sagittarians go the wrong way, when the opposition is too strong, when the odds are too heavy, when frustration too severe, you turn out like Basil Fawlty.

Youthful, Attractive

So you Sagittarians swing about the street through your teens, behaving noisily, clapping along, talking too loudly, boastfully looking after derelicts on the underground. With your Walkman playing the soundtrack directly into your brain you may come to believe that life out there is happening on a screen – it's all a multi-dimensional screen experience, and *you* are its hero. This translates into legal language as 'guilty but insane'.

You love speed, fast cars, dangerous driving, new girlfriends, drinks parties, parachuting and Formula One – it keeps you feeling young (about 14 ½). You travel, not to see the world, but to let the world see you (generosity comes easily). You are not intimidated by anything. Though you are unaware of your boisterous behaviour you are aggrieved when strangers insult you. Luckily you enjoy physical contact, in boxing and in sexual intercourse. You often join fights, on trains, in the street, and usually take the losing side (except in the sexual intercourse).

This pugnacity (which partly springs from your sense of justice) can be taken too far, and become self-destructive. After a short marriage your estranged wife may propose turning her divorce into the major profit-centre of her life with half your company, the rest of your capital and all your money. You Sagittarians resent this so much that you will go to jail for maintenance-arrears rather than pay, and bankrupt your limited company rather than sign over half of it to her.

But Rather Clumsy

Your sense of humour can be clumsy – especially when your hind quarters are responsible. However a surprising number of Sagittarian humorists were or are spokesmen for their generation. Sagittarian Billy Connolly was the triumph of his time, as much as Noel Coward and James Thurber were of theirs. The broad Scots comic also used many Sagittarian elements in his humour, notably the great play he found in 'big jobbies' – professional ground shared by fellow-Sagittarians Terry Gillam (scrap art and striking graphics of filth and violence), and Jonathan Swift.

Despite the fact that he looks as though he was caught standing over an exploding gas-tank, Mel Smith displays a more Libran subtlety in his talent (quiet, convincing, intelligent), confining his Sagittarian impulses to the dogtrack and driving his paisley-coloured Rolls Royce in and out of the Trent.

Paradoxically, Sagittarians seem to occupy the unattractive half of comedy duos – Ronnie Corbett, Ernie Wise and Syd Little, were all born under this Sign of the Centaur as indeed was *Lionel Blair!*

There may also be a melancholy, a yearning, a sense of spiritual loneliness underneath your comedic talents, as Sagittarian Joey 'Sir, I *Am* That Joey Grimaldi' Grimaldi shows us.

The Sagittarian Child

Dog-like.

Happy, playful Sagittarian children make no connection between brain and bowel until late in life; they leave great generous stools practically anywhere. Sometimes they are 52 before they learn.

Their candour gives them an advantage – especially on American game-shows. Fearlessness is an attractive trait, but an evolutionary dead end: fear is built in by our biology as a warning system, a proper respect for the larger and the hungrier (almost everyone, when you're 4 years old).

The Sagittarian Career

Your attitude to money is refreshingly contemptuous. You love to gamble, and often dabble in dogs, or stock, or dice games. It keeps you away from women, and this helps too.

Your technical vulgarity (the Tommy Steele touch, the Jonathan King kit, both classically awful Sagittarians) is often a help in dealing with life. You are also skilled at expressing anger – a vital metropolitan device, where at least half of your suppliers won't perform unless you shout at them. The worse you treat people the better they behave towards you (this only applies to professional relationships and relationships with a certain sort of woman).

Remember that you are likely to bring out the worst in your superiors. They become stuffier, more formal, more reserved, more meticulous, more anal – much more than they want to be. It is your wildness and weight that frighten them so. Make allowances for their doubting.

You do have ability, though, and you've only been fired by mistake, it's usually you who walks out. It infuriates your colleagues when you succeed (just frequently enough to keep your job secure), especially when you start saying, loudly, 'Well, whatever you think of me, at least I get the job done!'

Considering the way you behave – your frankness, your

boisterousness, your sexual effectiveness, the way you dismiss pretensions and unhealthy affectations, the way you puncture priggishness – it is amazing you do not have more enemies.

You are often successful in business, in spite of (perhaps because of) your explosive ego, which can go off like a scatter bomb, without warning. But you restlessly seek knowledge, and keep continuous updates of your data-base. And indeed, your lack of foresight is compensated occasionally by flashes of prophecy. However, this can enliven your curiosity ('Why? Why? Why? Why? Why? Why?') which sees you in your most tedious and insubordinate role. It is this trait that makes you unsuitable for services where unquestioning obedience, unfaltering solidarity is required. You can be strongly rebellious, and tend not to seek authority. You are too wild to lead effectively, except as a charismatic Christian. Even then, the times are too value-free for you to do very well – who knows Solzhenitsyn's phone number now?

Destroying The Sagittarian In The Boardroom

The flying hooves are a worry, but if you can get them flying, the Sagittarian will kick himself to death. To make him *really* angry question his integrity. Despite their reputation for straightforwardness, Sagittarians can be tremendously unconvincing: Nostradamus, Uri Geller, Margaret Meade begging for sex in Samoa, Lord Longford exercising his compassion in the House of Lords, Walt Disney whipping the original of Snow White in a bondage bar in Philadelphia – all of them Sagittarians, as little as they liked it.

So, suggest that his motives are tainted with self-interest; use his idealism against him, imply self-aggrandizement.

The Sagittarian is not good at strategy (though it doesn't hold them back, look at General Haig) – he doesn't need tactics (he just leaps over obstacles) and his peripheral vision isn't good enough for strategic assessments. He will cheerfully blunder into impossible situations, and then resign (and again, like General Haig, this will do wonders for his career).

Frame the Sagittarian by depositing fraudulent money in his building society. So incoherent with rage will he be that he won't be able to defend himself. And he will take the redundancy and run. Most Sagittarians don't stay to sue. And when they do, they lose.

The Successful Sagittarian

Sagittarians love low life, and to this end you remain as late bachelors, gamblers, street people, wanderers, cowboys, casual sex enthusiasts. Many of these characteristics are secondary homosexual characteristics; no wonder you are regarded cagily, outside the city. However, you do enjoy pubs and betting shops and unreliable jobs, and long odds.

For many of these reasons, you can end up much richer and more powerful than those around you. Because you are unfettered and unafraid, because you don't hesitate to pursue your self-interest, because your stature is that much greater than your competitors, you have a far better chance of cracking the big ones. You are not too busy earning a living to achieve wealth.

You are helped in this by a soaring imagination. You are not a dreamer, like the Piscean. You are a Fire sign, but as the most advanced Fire sign your ideas are the most practical, the most powerful, and you have the most amount of weight to back them up. The ideas are frequently good – the speed at which you habitually move means that you look at everything as an outsider, and this gives you a valuable perspective. Neither do you flinch from putting your hand on a financier's knee, look him in the eye and promise you can make it happen for him. Your abilities in the matter of seduction are most appreciated in the City. You also benefit from what seems to be an unnatural amount of *luck*. You walk around attracting good fortune, and considering your personality, and the way you behave, this is incredible.

You can also end up dead, much more quickly than other signs. Because you are so *lucky* you may not get killed in the avalanche – but your need for living dangerously will take you too close to the edge, where the others were swept away, and many of you will eventually go over yourselves.

At best you are a godlike creature. A Victor Ludorum; brains, beauty, captain of everything and winner of the Mrs Joyful Prize for Raffia Work. It is a shame so few of you ever get out of your teens.

Sagittarius In Love

> When I saw ladies in my dreams I called them pretty mother, but when one actually came to me, I shot her.
>
> *Peter Pan*

Sagittarians display the classic pathology of the Peter Pan syndrome – a fear of growing out of childishness into the network of social and emotional responsibilities. Your very strength – free-ranging, independent, soaring imagination – is to preserve yourself against this commitment. To this end you often take refuge behind your self-proclaimed honesty, using it to defuse embarrassing moments of sexual intimacy ('Getting a bit fat old girl, need to take in a bit of drape at the back').

If you take a girlfriend to a party you will leave her with your coat and not talk to her until you both leave. If you don't leave together you may never talk to her again, no matter how many flowers you send.

Women say to you 'You don't want an equal relationship with a proper woman, you just want some silly dolly bird saying how fantastic you are all the time!' All women say that to men, but in your case there is just cause.

Half-Man, Half-Horse

Women who are successful with you give you a great deal of rope. They give you room, they give you freedom, so much so that they never see you again – they are the lucky ones. You like to have girlfriends more than lovers (though they have to come across, of course), and you find no difficulty in arranging this, as your large, beachboy body is attractive to a certain sort of girl. And you are genuinely friendly to them. You just need them to allow you to walk away from them in the middle of the street, in the middle of the night, in the middle of a gynaesophical act saying, 'I think I'll go and get Venetia. I'll see you tomorrow.'

You are large and unsentimental. People lodge their affections in you, not realizing that you cruise. Girls may ride you for a while, but you develop saddle sores. They may ride you bareback for a little longer, but steady company is often irksome for the young Sagittarian

Half-Man, Half-Dog

The fact is you are promiscuous, you are a slut, you whang it about, anything that moves, and if it's warm – twice. Jumping and pumping, bumping and dumping, you have a lot of sexual confidence, an enormous appetite for infidelity and, very often, a venereal infection. Your tongue hangs out, you pant, you squirm, you strip women naked and wriggle around on top of them, you make a mess of the bed, you growl and grovel, you slobber and lick, and it's just as well or you wouldn't have any women friends at all.

But you know that you are a sexual predator. You seize women and roll them over, you raid them for sexual information – though you have updated your database with it already. These serial relationships offer you the same data again and again. You haven't had many sexual experiences: you've had the same sexual experience many times.

Half-Man, Half-Pig

The fear of intimacy, which is the other side of your rangeroving personality causes you to say deliberately bruising things to those who threaten you with intimacy, especially when they're slipping under your duvet. 'How do you find that HM loo paper? Enough grip for you?'

Women compliment you on the large size of your sexual organ. You may be so stupid that you return the compliment. You want her to wonder whether it is all worth it. This is a successful strategy of yours, one of the few.

In Marriage

You do not accept the natural rights of mothers-in-law to come in and make hay of your marriage, and this can cause domestic friction. As can your sports-conscious spare time. And your contemptuous attitude to money. And the way you leave the bathroom ('*Sickening*, do you hear? Running around after you cleaning up is *sickening!*')

Your restless pathology leads you to the top of the divorce charts. Your attitude to marriage is fluid (yours is a mutable sign, you want to communicate, not to lead, and what you communicate is that you want a divorce).

On the good side – because you are accustomed to saying what you think, and even more, what you feel, you are not a victim of the frustration that produces violence. You generally open doors before passing through them, and break plates before you throw them. Your wife says, 'You *never* do *anything* you don't *want* to!' as you slug it out for ownership. But then all wives say that to their husbands.

Who's My Girl! Who's My Big Red Girl!

Your red setter.

Women

Sagittarian women are quite without pretension – this is your single largest failing. A very small sense of snobbery would stop your exuberant drinking and all the social humiliation that stems from it.

You have large, powerful limbs, and men sense the vigour beneath your clothes. The rhythm of your legs, the swing of your stride, attracts the unwary. They are drawn to the smell of your hair, and the sense of freedom in your dress-sense, no less than the speed with which you let men see you naked. You canter across the landscape confidently, cheerfully, with a variety of riders on your back, knocking some people down, throwing others off. However, you are tremendously loyal, and always will keep up with old friends, no matter how decrepit, stupid, poor they become ('It must be awfully dull coming to see me, dear,' they say. 'Oh it *is!*' you cheerfully reply).

Motor Mouth

Sagittarian women can be unbearably communicative, leaping into a conversation as if released from a starting stall. You clear a path for your argument with flying hooves. You can also clear the room, and this disappoints a party-minded creature such as yourself ('Hi gang!'). Be careful though – strangers can take advantage of your beaming guilelessness to use you as an introduction to your team, and then drop you. Not that you'll mind much, even if you notice. The truth is, you are too taken with your own perceptions to be *very* interested in the complicated dishonesty of those around you.

Outspoken

You open your mouth and out it comes. Ideas comes to you with a physical force, they explode in your brain and are expressed at once ('Her hand flew to her mouth, but too late! The horse had bolted!'). Intuitive flashes make hay of any good intentions you may have of courteous reticence. 'This man is an idiot,' and 'This man has an extremely small penis' are ideas that will be given excited expression at any time, in any company.

Enormous Abilities

Perhaps it is the duality inherent in the centaur symbol of your sign, but you have a deep need to be doing two things at once, one with your top half and another with your bottom, and this can create complications. But you are versatile – the fact that you need novelty urges you ever into pastures new. You are a party girl, cruising for a good time, but looking back you may wonder how good a time it has been. Not that you do look back. 'Never look back,' you say with certainty (your conservative nature is drawn to the security of awful clichés). You don't look back as you may see something gaining on you (possibly one of your ex-husbands, or a family you deserted when you were poor).

This free-ranging impulse leads you into unfamiliar situations. It is your greatest asset. The mixed bag of your experience provokes peculiar data combinations, new and exciting patterns of energy. This gives you a reputation for personal liberation and taking your clothes off at parties – but you are nonetheless deeply conservative (except in matters of sex), and you yearn for obedience.

Musical

Your ear for music is quick, and your generous nature may encourage you in a role of patron of the arts. You are expansive, and expensive. With your boisterous manner and frankly sensual regard, you are the sort of patron artists most dread. Though you have the talent to be artistically accomplished, you so underalue the talent ('Scribbling, picking out a tune on the old ivories, daubing away at the old still lives') that you rarely come to much.

Sexually

You're a cheerful girl to strip yourself so quickly, and you often star in the locker-room conversation of your male acquaintance. (They don't really like it when you say 'Wanna come up and play with my toys?' At parties, you ask men 'Wanna play gynaecologists?' and even though many of the heavier types you favour do come across, your large manner does frighten them, no matter what they say.) You are an adventurer and are much given to exploratory sex – it saddens you how little there is to explore, when it actually comes down to it: oral sex, anal sex, nasal sex feature in your experience, or at least your fantasies, and though you may explore every crease and fold of flesh for its possibilities, you can often feel there is something missing, and you venture into theatrical elements. Things can get really rough at this stage. You have a good sexual memory, and every bout of congress adds data – typically, Sagittarians have the biggest sexual databases in the Zodiac, but the retrieval system is uncertain. When your sexual systems are switched on almost anything can happen – it may not be comfortable, but at least it shows you are alive. You believe in the joyousness of sex – men are surprised when you yodel. An overhead view of the bed shows you kicking breaststroke with your legs during intercourse, and it is not unusual for you to swim off in the middle.

Sex with a Sagittarian can be an overwhelming experience for men, so make allowances for them – they liken it to acquiring carnal knowledge of a tumble dryer, especially when you make use of specialized wrestling holds (you are often a *large* women). You usually win the first encounters (surprise is on your side, and the first strike is decisive – men worry that you won't respect them in the morning), but as your partner becomes more experienced it may get messy. Submissions take second place to knockouts, particularly when he tries to take you roughly from behind in the kitchen.

Paradoxically, you long, deep down, to be released from your independent nature, to submit to someone else, to be tamed, to wear saddlery and tack and to be jockeyed round the drawing room making little whinnying noises as he marks you with his crop. The feeling is not common, and often does not last – your mate will look foolish when you abandon him for your normal self, so be prepared for a tremendous right cross when you do.

You are serious about sex. Somewhere that you cannot quite reach in your mind there is the knowledge that you can canter the phallus into open country, out under a sky of strangely brilliant blue and unfamiliar stars. You feel you can fight through the flesh, though the jungle of blood and drugs to be reborn into a world of light and turning silence.

You need a strong man, or a very, very stupid one.

In some awful cases you can be a real *dog* (*vide* Jane Fonda).

The Sagittarians

Lord Lucan, Vasco da Gama, Ian Botham, General de Gaulle, Hoagy Carmichael, John Bird and Derek Jameson, Harpo Marx, Diana Quick, Toulouse-Lautrec, Andrew Carnegie, Lord Forte, Pat Phoenix, Ernie Wise, Caroline Kennedy, William Blake, Busby Berkeley, Terry Gilliam, Tom Conti, Sir Peter Hall, Group Captain Peter Townsend, Benjamin Britten, Lew Hoad, Sir Peter Strawson, Billy Connolly, David Kossoff, Alun Owen, Grace Darling, Francis Durbridge, John Kennedy Jr, Imran Khan, Tina Turner, John Alderton, Rodney Bews, Robert Dougall, Lord Howard de Walden, Verity Lambert, Hey Jimi Hendrix, Nancy Mitford, Randy Newman, Jacques Chirac, John Mayall, Charles Hawtrey, Frank Ifield, Efrem Zimbalist Jr, Palladio, Sir Winston Churchill, Mark Twain, Jonathan Swift, Woody Allen, Keith Michell, Mary Martin, Bette Midler, Matt Monroe, Gilbert O'Sullivan, Richard Prior, Andy Ripley, Lee Trevino, General Haig, Julie Harris, Jean-Luc Godard, Mel Smith, Ronnie Corbett, Jimmy Jewel, Gemma Jones, Dr A.L. Rowse, Pamela Stephenson, Edith Cavell, General Franco, Maria Callas, Lord Chalfont, Lord Longford, Lord Maffews, Sheridan 'Oh God' Morley, Otto Preminger, Walt Disney, David Brubeck, Sir Osbert Sitwell, Ellen Burstyn, Beethoven, Noel Coward, Jane Austen, Joey Grimaldi, Noam Chomsky, Eli

Wallach, Julian Critchley, Sammy Davis Jr, Lord Diplock, Lucian Freud, James Galway, Sibelius, James Thurber, Joan Armatrading, John Cassavetes, Judi Dench, Kirk 'Silly Old Fool' Douglas, Hermione Gingold, Donny Osmond, Elizabeth Schwarzkopf, John Milton, Benny Green, Rumer Godden. Brenda Lee, Cliff 'Sunday Afternon In East Berlin' Michelmore, Christina Onassis, the dreadful, dreadful, dreadful Lionel Blair, Connie Francis, Ed Koch, John 'One Shot' Osborne, Emperor Roscoe, Frank Sinatra, Dionne Warwick, Lord Bullock, Anouska Hempel, Christopher Plummer, Sir Laurens van der Post, Lee Remick, Rosemary Sutcliff, Nostradamus, Tycho Brahe, Michael Bogdanov, Dave Clark, Edna O'Brien, Nero, J. Paul Getty, Arthur C. Clarke, Joel Garner, Liv Ullman, Christopher Cazenove, Bernard Hill, Kerry Packer, Robert Robinson, Tommy Steele, Willy Brandt, Eammon Andrews, Gordon Jackson, Saki, Paul Klee, Syd Little, Jenny Agutter, Bo Derek, Irene Dunne, Uri Geller, Rachel Trickett, Jane Fonda, Edith Piaff, Sir John Barbirolli, Deanna Durbin, Clarence Birds-eye, Alexander Solzhenitsyn, Dick van Dyke, King George VI, Frank Zappa and the Piltdown Man.

CAPRICORN

22 December – 20 January

The Glyph

Capricorn is symbolized by the Goat, the least attractive beast in the Zodiac. Anyone who has tasted goat will not be surprised at that animal's solitary habits.

It is not just the animal's hygienic economy that drives it out of society. The mode of the Goat is a climbing one, and those born under the Goat are driven to ever-higher things. Capricorns love to look down on their fellows, insects in the distance, with a profound sense of superiority. The goat-purpose of their ascent is not clear. Perhaps for spiritual ambition, or perhaps for social authority; quite often just for better gossip.

However, it is never for the Zen pleasure of climbing, and in this we see the fatal flaw in the Capricorn character.

Your Ruling Planet

Capricorn is ruled by Saturn, and in this we find much that we would rather not. Saturn is the planet of deferred gratification. Saturn offers the spirit of the Scottish Presbyterian Church. It is a planet of cold charity, corporal punishment and strict construction. A harsh, dour, tight, hairshirted planet. A lot of death is connected with it, and arthritis, and authority, and housemasters. It is tight underclothes and self-denial; Saturn is that which we fear. The long dreariness of the planet's shadow can darken large and vital areas of the Capricorn's personality, and it is this which is responsible for your success in life, though only with your bank manager.

The planet has had an unaccountably bad press over the centuries, but is enjoying some rehabilitation in the eighties. Its strictness is suited to the times. As the winter cold is necessary for germination, so Saturnine discipline is needed for new growth. Though what new growth ever came of arthritis is hard to say.

Men And Women: The Capricorn Personality

You take pride in your bewilderment at food processors, quantum theory, computer games, ionizers, credit cards, personal stereos, hair conditioners, air-conditioners, central heating, psycho-active drugs, therapy, psycho-analysis, auto-redial telephones, dictaphones, and remote channel changes for the television. And television.

Yours is the sign of Victorian values – thrift, self-improvement, regular bowel habits, the Queen's peace, sensible shoes, your own front door and a little truckle bed. The twentieth century invention you admire most is the choke chain. You always know where your tube ticket is (in your glove), you always turn down the thermostat (if you even have central heating), and you are always complacent for the return of capital punishment (if only for those who advocate capital punishment). You believe in *consequences* and revenge as an element of justice. You favour sound money, old-fashioned manners, and the humiliation of the spendthrift by taking their family away and putting them into what you scornfully call 'care'. You find The Nanny State an insult to human dignity ('It turns perfectly good manpower into Irishmen').

Self-sufficiency is your ambition, self-help, self-interest.

Self-awareness is not one of your strong points (Elvis Presley's lack of self-awareness was responsible for his Capricorn death at twenty-two stone). You feel you are tremendously well organized. You lay out elements of your personality as if for kit inspection, but the unexamined contents of certain ancestral wardrobes do not make a pretty sight. In this new age of Mrs Thatcher's Second Coming you may feel triumphantly justified in your Saturnine attitudes towards the weak, the useless, the unappealing ('*Someone's* got to be practical!'), but there is a complex knottiness in your apparent straightforwardness, there is a darkness in your clear ideas, and we will come to find this sinister.

The avant garde of the provisional Right Wing (Alexander Chancellor, Peregrine Worsthorne, P.W. Botha, John Junor, Bernard Shrimsley and Kenny Everett) is hardcore Capricorn. You thoroughly approve of incentives for the workers (if they don't work hard enough you fire them), and consistent with this you agitate for incentives to management (abolition of women's minimum wages, NIC, and personal income tax over thirty per cent). Barry Goldwater, and J. Edgar Hoover (who wanted Negroes to be compelled to wear choke chains), were triumphant examples of the sign. As indeed was Al Capone, who beat twelve tied employees to death with a single baseball bat. Idi Amin is a Capricorn. Of course all Capricorns hate Arthur Scargill, except Scargill himself who perfectly exemplifies the sign's monotonous intolerance and its way of casting the world in its own image. The personality suffers from a lack of proper ventilation, and this must become unhealthy. There is something remote and finally unattractive about members of this sign, something doctrinaire, obdurate, impenetrable. Something rather dead.

Your Tight Hold On Death

Your profoundly habitual personality gives an insight to the morbidity to which you are subject. It is something to do with the awful old cardigan you feel so comfortable in, and the old jokes you drag out again and again, your old mental clothes, your changeless mind.

You re-run whole conversations with strangers, word for word, you are a genuine oral tradition, but more in the manner of a tape player than a story teller. You have one quip for foreigners ('Everyone makes mistakes said the hedgehog to the hairbrush,' which you trot out in your awful Edward Heath French, even to Germans). Spontaneity makes you anxious. Any innovation makes you anxious. Anxiety frightens you. This is why you are so conservative: things have to last because you cannot adapt. You use the same restaurant, the same holiday resort year after year even though you don't like it! *Even though you have never liked it!* The security of dismal familiarity outweighs the anxiety of uncertain pleasure.

The vitality of the Capricorn fossilizes early. Your outer layers harden, like lava. Very soon you end up looking, and maybe even sounding, like Capricorn Bernard Cribbins. Now your life, your molten self exists deep down, very privately, a long way away from the fresh air and free intercourse of the living. Displays of emotion (especially grief and affection) you find deeply frightening ('Pass the sickbag, Alice'). No wonder you say, 'It's a long life and a grey one,' to anyone still listening.

If you were more alive you would be aware of the pain and the sadness of life; how days flicker and are gone; you would know how everything falls apart, love fails and children die; you would know about the carnage of married life, and loneliness in the darkening days; your mother giving birth astride a grave; the soaring mortgages, the pound continuing to fall. You would know these things, and actually draw a pleasantly morbid satisfaction from them, but either you daren't, or you can't escape from the neo-cortical abstraction you have constructed for yourself. You can't go down into that part of you that is still quick. The plaque is impenetrable. The horror you sense inside yourself (Capricorn Janet Street Porter) is quite enough for you, without exploring the horror of life outside (Capricorns Janis Joplin, the Duke of Devonshire, Aristotle Onassis).

You end up, by an administrative anomaly, lonelier than you'd like, in the aisles of the Europa stores, a bottle of wine-type EEC drinking fluid in your wire basket, a place at your polished mahogany table, laid for one.

So You Hang On To

Your career.

The Capricorn Career

You Capricorns are astoundingly ambitious. You may not give it away, your modest manners and careful sense of debt and duty may conceal it, but you are the most ambitious sign of the Zodiac. More Lords (Acton to Wheatley, as well as Jack Lord of Hawaii Five-O) began life under Capricorn than any other.

So remember – if your ambition is not exercised, that part of the personality will turn cancerous, and resentment will devour the whole. You feel you have to prevail, on whatever terms. You will sacrifice anything to do so, particularly yourself (something you are rather good at).

Because you feel that work is all there is, you work too hard, driving yourself. You work to build something you can rely on, something that will offer you the illusion of permanence and safety. Thus money and property, law and order, mean more to you than happiness ('*Happi*ness? But who ever expected to be *happy?*')

But Success Is Many Things

So important is it to you to win that if you can't win you won't play. However, if you have time to prepare youself for defeat you can be a graceful loser, because the craven part of you wants, the dead part of you wants, the commodity vital to you: admiration.

You have to be admired.

Admiration is an absolute requirement for you. Not to be liked ('I'm not running a popularity contest'), but to be respected. Without respect and admiration you wither. And the sad fact is that you are not good at attracting admiration (Roy Hattersley, Walter Mondale, Cliff Thorburn). Richard Nixon (whose career was a perfect expression of remorseless Capricorn ambition) showed in his 1962 speech of Presidential defeat at the hands of Kennedy ('. . . no one will support him more than me . . .') the dark side of this submissive posture.

Your need to be on the winning side also draws you into formal conservatism – it is the best vantage point from which to look down on the ignorance, the idleness and the impotence of the rest of society. You are boastfully out of fashion. You are so conservative you still are not used to seeing black men driving motorcars. The respect for authority which you display comes from this admiration of winners. So Capricorns will patiently tolerate injustice (unless you are directly affected yourself) in the name of preserving the Queen's peace – disorder you see as a sort of general injustice. The orderly queue is a source of deep satisfaction; the orderly dole-queue makes you positively cheerful.

The apparatus of the state deeply impresses you. You succeed because you understand the system as only its deepest admirers can – it all makes sense to you, anything from curfews, to the Lord Chancellor, to TV game show hosts. You bow to the wisdom of better men than yourself. This, of course, is the first condition necessary for Nazi consciousness. Indeed, your fear and dislike of anyone who is different from you (especially Jews and gypsies) the relentlessness of your purpose, your tight fist, the low thermostat, the one telephone in the cold hall, the protective plaque you build up round your soul all combine to make you vulnerable to totalitarian sympathies. You do particularly well in IBM.

Getting Your Own Way

You are a very 1980s negotiator in that you do not negotiate. You state your case and stick to it in the face of all contradiction. If a clever Capricorn you may vary the vocabulary, even the syntax, but you will be inflexible, unassailable. It is not in your nature to reach out to yourself to compromise. This helps your reputation for reliability. You are also able, in moments of inspiration, to accuse your oppoinents of intransigence (Arthur Scargill again).

As a talented worrier you are also equipped to plot the course of a strategy with commendable pessimism (you can be known to collapse under an anxiety attack when the news is good).

The worldliness with which you were aparently born can too easily degenerate into cynicism. Much of your knowledge of human nature can be reduced to the proposition that men can make more on the supplementary benefit than they can working.

However, you are a meticulous administrator; cold and suspicious, and this is your strong suit. You excel in your relationship with a contract. You do nothing recklessly. There is something sinister about the speed at which you move. Like a nightmare coming from behind, you approach across sinking ground. Nothing stops you. The only thing that prevents you from reaching the very top is that you move at the speed of a World War I tank. You may not be manoevrable (Cassius Clay an interesting exception), but you are inexorable.

You do outstandingly well in corporate life, though your reluctance to move ('Abroad is bloody and all foreigners are fiends') and your company loyalty will hold you back from the large, fast rewards. Just as you are careful managing your own money you are careful with other peoples', and this may prevent you ever making much yourself. But you have a major talent at organizing yourself as the still centre of a turning world. It pleases you deeply to see younger, more energetic men performing to your music.

As A Writer

Though you are not normally drawn to self-employment, your deficiencies as a team player push you into this solitary habit. You operate too secretly for cooperation, preferring a steady singles game (often playing both sides of the net, as only writers can).

The appeal of this occupation lies in the fact that you can create a world absolutely on your own terms. A world in which you are not contradicted or criticized. J.R.R. Tolkien was a particularly unsettling example of this (the *scale* of his books being so absurd). You can enter this neo-cortical abstraction and be completely secure (though increasingly poor). Nothing here happens without your permission. Your powerful, if damaged, imagination comes into its own.

Only as a writer can you allow your secret vitality out to animate your characters – they may not move very far but they move where you tell them. As with your children, your employees and your submissive sexual partners, you keep your fictional creations tight on their choke chains, and this may have a morbid effect on their animation. Everything you are successful with turns out looking like you. At first you will be pleased by this, but it may not always be so. It is easy to become bored with the close company of yourself. Disenchantment is dangerous for the Capricorn. It gathers like a dense depression at the base of the brain, a feeling like an impenetrable hangover which prevents you from making contact with the outside world. Though you are tenacious of life this feeling can result in a total psychic collapse late in life – very much a mixed blessing.

In worldly terms your hunger for recognition will be satisfied, given that you find success, and this may justify for you the enormous anxieties of the self-employed: recognition and real estate being what you most want in the world, prose and property.

But In The End

All ambition is empty, and you should realize this, though it will probably be too late. You may be dying before you realize money is crap.

Money is a cold comfort. And the security it offered never gave you pleasure. Like heroin, money merely relieved your anxieties; like dangerous drugs, it merely made you feel normal.

If you realize this in time, however, it may signal a radical change of life for you – it will be painful for you to be unreliable in your late middle age but it may well be your one chance for redemption.

Health

There is some arthritis in your astrology, and harsh black stools may shear off haemorrhoids late in life, but otherwise you enjoy good health ('Rude good health,' you call it).

How You Get On In The Eighties

You are well suited to scarcity; rationing agrees with you, it allows you to exercise your talent for self-denial, scavenging, skimping, making do, ruining your eyes darning socks by the light of the *Daily Telegraph*.

After the seventies (you were very unhappy with the seventies – the terrifying inflation, the lack of unemployment, the ragbag of wishful mythology that passed for political thought) you feel more at home. You take unrestrained market forces as a much more reliable indicator of economic health than anything the do-gooding entrepreneurs of compassion ever came up with. Pain you find a much more reliable master than pleasure. You may rather not be there, but at least you know where you are. You're also much more confident about things you don't like than things you do.

It will take a lot more uncertainty in the currency, and a little more confirmation that we are not on the winning side of the market forces, to persuade you that intervention is ideologically acceptable. Unemployment will have to rise to seven million to persuade you of the same thing.

Making A Mess Of The Capricorn

Because he is so tight and tactical it will be difficult to get the Capricorn to reveal anything of himself to you, until you are in no position to harm him (he will know more about you at any given time than you do about him). The Capricorn will not confide, or gossip, or reveal his weakness. This makes it difficult to get to him.

As he is so reliable, you have to rattle him into making a mistake, and this is not easy – he is also capable. There are three weaknesses that may be useful:

1 He is much more sensitive to criticism than he appears. Remember his longing for respect and admiration. Beneath his taciturn, self-sufficient exterior he yearns for approval. Your criticisms will not be acknowledged, but may prepare ground conditions favourable for a pre-strike situation. You will have to rattle him to make him behave badly. Although he looks fearlessly in control remember his deep anxieties.

2 His job has a religious significance. Monthly deposits in his checking account he sees as a form of secular communion. Job security is his salvation. He has a relationship with his nest egg, like mad people have.

3 There are always opportunities for explosive progress that the Capricorn will discount. He will object on principle, even when the rewards are huge – *especially* when the rewards are huge – and usually he is correct. Sure things are rare birds. You must make him jump. He can always justify his conservative stance, even when it loses out – you must use his ambition, greed, and fear of public opinion to push him out into the new technology where he may collapse under the weight of his own anxieties.

The Love Of A Capricorn Man

You Capricorn men cannot believe in anything you cannot understand, and this has a morbid effect on your relations with the opposite sex. You approach the mystery of women with all the flair of a chief petty officer. For Christmas you buy a back-pack, a spice-rack, a box of chocolates for a wife on a diet, and you marvel at their boot-faces. Your essential shyness does not help your need to be admired, especially in your dealings with compliments (What's their game? What are they after? Will you have to compliment them back? Don't they know how much you hate to be in debt?).

Capricorns rarely fall in love, and when you do it is not a happy experience for either party. The defences are intricate and substantial (which is just as well). You never give yourself away. Always, a policeman-like exterior is maintained. Maximum security is your passion. Only hippies (or beatniks as you call them) squander their emotional substance, scatter their seed, splash about themselves with their feelings. You are immensely cautious with your emotions, as with your money (very often they are the same thing). Prospective partners must pass through the fine mesh of your requirements. It is a very fine mesh.

Thus your romantic targets have to crack a highly subtle code, a succession of twelve imperceptible signals beamed backwards and forwards in precisely the right sequence. Each beat in the exchange is crucial – if the wrong move is made by either party the whole process has to start again at lunch (anything up to a week later). The difficult thing is that you rarely give any indication the exchange is taking place. The odds against anyone successfully completing it are 12,554,489 to 1. You are saddened by the small number of people prepared to dedicate so many lunch hours to a pre-courtship.

Love strikes as a very rare frenzy, and it is not a pleasant feeling. The lack of self-control frightens you, the sense of failing autonomy, falling walls, the sense of anxiety and defeat. You liken the physical sensation to some large insect crawling through your lungs, laying its eggs.

How Is A Girl To Tell?

If you like the look of a Capricorn man and you want to know whether he likes the look of you – take off your clothes and look at yourself in the mirror. If you have long legs and slim hips, and the top of you inner thighs kiss when you shift your weight; if your lower lip swells and pouts, and looks wet when your tongue moves in your mouth; if your eyelids droop over almond shaped eyes; if you push your hair back out of your eyes, and shake your head as you do; if your breasts move as you lean forward but are still firm, and the swell of your stomach falls to your auburn hair, and the cradle of your thighs, if your parents are rich . . . you may assume the Capricorn likes the look of you.

You may get contradictory signals, but he still likes the look of you: even when he calls an after-dinner cab for you, even when you get him to Paris and he bolts for the airport, even when you are naked and he is breathing heavily before suddenly disappearing, it is just his way of saying how he wants you. He hasn't found the right words yet.

Capricorn's Best Targets

As a Capricorn you may not be a clinical sadist but you do like masochists.

A girl who openly admires you, who subjugates herself to your will, who vibrates in tune to your voice, who shows a hunger for degradation at your hands, who buys her own slave-bracelets for you, is half way to your heart. Her obedience causes your tumescence.

The choke chain (by far the most appropriate symbol for this sign) keeps her under control, reduces her strike capability, makes her safe for your attentions.

Women always say, at some point in a relationship, 'You don't want an equal relationship with a proper woman, you just want some silly dolly bird saying how fantastic you are all the time.' But when she says it to you Capricorns, she is right.

The idea of an equal relationship fills you with depression and difficulty. The enthusiastic masochist is what you want, however damaged or complicated she is.

Even in love, *especially* in love, the Capricorn feels himself to be vulnerable to attack, treachery, subversion. This is why you are so discreet, so shy about what it is you are after (and rightly so). Surprised girls suddenly find themselves over your knee, or tied to the architecture of the bed, or upside-down in the dirty linen basket. They should never complain, for fear of losing you – it takes very little to put you off, particularly when you feel a reasonable man would not happily be photographed by the *News Of The World* in this posture.

Sexually

You often have a substantial sexual apparatus which, by a trick of business, increases with your commercial success (if Britt Ekland is to be believed this does not apply to Capricorn Rod Stewart).

Your stern, rather starved exterior makes you awkward with the opposite sex. Your sex life can be sparse – you set so many tests that all those who eventually qualify have generally lost interest. As an obsessive, emotional cripple, you find difficulty enjoying sex, slung, as you are, in the traction of your insurance premiums.

Intercourse, when mechanically successful, is a melancholy business coloured by your pre-coital tristesse. The sadness starts on penetration of the mystery. In the million points of contact entering her citadel, you sense a society you can never share. You build this into a general theory of impotence. You come to believe nothing lasts, that nothing is real, emotions come and go, pleasure fades, desire fails. Your tragedy that you are not looking for love, you are looking for company stock, you're looking for something you can keep in a safe – this sexual intercourse is all a philosophical category mistake. The commerce is illusory, the product a futures fantasy, and the currency is in Monopoly money.

No wonder you are sad.

Sex is where men can show themselves to be most alive. Your hold on death is usually too strong. No wonder you can be overwhelmed with weariness – so tired of your own company, never making contact with the outside world because you cannot make contact with yourself. And you get depressed. It is a shame your anti-Keynsian nature prevents you from spending your way out of the depression.

The Theatrical Element

It is no coincidence that the cockney slang of J. Arthur Rank was born under Capricorn. Sensing the anxiety that improvisation causes you, your lover will learn your sexual texts and follow them, word-perfect.

Instinctively she must deduce that the anxiety which free intercourse rouses in you leads you to prefer the act to be externalized, dramatized. To be laid out as a script, formally, with stage directions and dialogue given. Just to be practical, she will hear you say, when the act is about to begin. Just so that you both know what you are doing.

It is the beginning of Capricorn voyeurism. You lead the conversation round to the discipline at her school, to her experience of lesbianism, to her taste in restrictive clothing. If you cannot watch her doing it with someone else (the perfect compromise) then talking about her doing it with someone else has a powerful appeal. The only misgiving she may have is to find out you have been working on these texts since you were six years old.

It has been your practice to rehearse them and re-rehearse them – it's your game, they are your rules, and if she won't play you play by yourself. Even if she does play, you still play by yourself (it takes her some time – months, perhaps years – to realize this). She may be disappointed to find that any variation spoils the act, any spontaneity spoils it, any sign of life spoils it. But this is tough tuna.

Regular Habits

On the positive side: you may not be very satisfactory, but at least you continue well into middle age. Women who use the act for reassurance continue to be reassured, and this is good.

Very Rare Frenzy

On very rare occasions life can imitate art so closely that your text may be spontaneously acted out by an unknowing collaborator. Be warned: this is a dangerous situation. Your circuits will overload. The wiring will fuse. Your brain will blow up. As the victim of sexual breakdown you will sit in front of the television with a rug over your knees, an invalid, for months, possibly forever.

In Marriage

You do not feed your wife with what she really wants (uninterrupted sexual intercourse and expressions of your lively feelings). You even begrudge her the continental footwear and her very modest dress allowance. But you then do provide her with a *very* comfortable home, and a *more* than adequate sum for housekeeping. This regular home-life offers an appearance of emotional security, but you easily confuse emotional security with emotional sloth. You are always out of step, and respond to your spouse *late*, if you respond at all. You only move when you are certain of your ground: your wife takes this, rightly, to be a lack of trust between you. You can live, like a lizard, on a very dry diet.

However, you can be fair, and are unfailingly courteous. Especially when you realize how these qualities can hinder successful marital intercourse. In the long, hard negotiation of married life you will learn to keep a poker face to strike the best terms. Your bargaining style is meticulous, detailed, inch-by-inch. The less you give away, the less your spouse has to go on, the less power she has over you. It's a waiting game you play. Not until later do you realize it is death you are waiting for.

In the first years your spouse may have some ambition to come close to you, but the scorched earth policy of the fierce and frightened Capricorn effectively deters her. You will burn off, and replant some years later on a modest basis – a formal sort of marriage, companionable but not passionate, a comfortable sense of mutual solitude, an undemanding sofa life, a domestic policy of separate development, not *married* as such, but loosely federated under the Matrimonial Property Act.

Your ear becomes quickly dulled to the sawing voices of dissatisfied women.

Women

You are most frequently seen complaining to the supervisor. You are frightened of life, but not of sales staff – this is your finest quality (and being objective, as Capricorn women are, it's really not very fine, as qualities go, is it?). Mornings are bad for you, and so are afternoons. About half an hour after your first drink is a good time (it lasts about nine minutes), assuming you drink, which many Capricorns don't.

You are vaguely disapproving throughout your life. You say it's because you're a perfectionist, but there is a sinister element in perpetual criticism. You are always found underneath, checking for leaks, boils, scabs, spots, your fingers are busy parting hair, lifting arms, spreading flesh to get a closer and more complete look at it. No wonder your children leave home as soon as they can (round about the time they can walk). You bleed freely from the nose when hit. Even when you are overwhelmed with satisfaction you feel you will have lost points if you don't find something to complain about. 'Oh yes, I like the house well enough, but why did you buy those *hideous* vegetable racks, and blue binliners? Really? *Blue bin-liners?* And the paintwork in the bathroom cupboards is *filthy* and I'm *sure* I've no idea when the rubbish is collected.' This will upset those close to you, especially if they've paid for the house: but you will not know why they're upset, even if they tell you.

If you rebel early in life you will be the first to punish yourself, and later you will build this into a general theory of social relations. When young you probably knew two canes – a gentler called Spaniel, and a fiercer called Greyhound. You will apply them to others as they were applied to you. Your great sense of justice means that you will give as good as you get, though not necessarily to the same people, and this is why you are unhappy in life.

In Your Career

As an office person you provide a cost-effective commercial service, and in a well-run company your critical talents will be underemployed: you will be less happy but more popular. However, in a creative environment you will suffer distress – the noise, the people, the level of music (*'Would you mind turning that down, thank you?'*) It's not just the cans of beer on the desks, it's more the legs of the typists waving in the air as the copy yobs enter them from above. You find that unnecessary – 'Nobody thinks it's clever, nobody thinks you're funny,' you may say to the sluts as they adjust their dress and their make-up in the staff lavatories, 'And why do you wear make-up down there? It's not amusing you know, it really isn't.'

You don't last long there, and go back to whatever accountant's office you left last.

Telling Jokes To Capricorn Women

You are cut off from humanity by your sense of humour. You don't see what's funny about it – 'What's pink and wrinkled and hangs out your trousers? That isn't funny, it's just disgusting.' You still don't find it funny, even when they chorus at you, 'Your mother, your mother, that's what's pink and wrinkled and hangs out your trousers.' You just look tired; 'But it isn't funny, it's just disg—Oh I seeeeee—but that isn't funny? Is it? Why is that funny?'

As a wife you were condemned in a Diplock court of matrimony to a life sentence of penile servitude. So you say. At least you can regulate it – often by covering your entire body with an inch of Nivea – to 'once a week on Saturday, with no mucking about'. You are known to nudge your daughter on the way to church and say, with a tight little smile, 'You can ask the old man for anything today.' The Nivea trick is not always successful, and your laundry bills can be enormous. So can your sense of revulsion, and you may not talk to the brute for three weeks. A Libran woman under the same circumstances would be in sexual ecstasy.

Enough is enough for you, sexually, and it really isn't very much compared with the carnivores of the Zodiac. You worry too much about trivial things to enjoy sex – your Barclaycard account keeps you out of your body on some peculiar plane of existence. And your objective sense, your talent for criticism, is so strong that it never really goes on stand-by, even during congress – you may suddenly remark with a bell-like clarity 'You're actually very clumsy in many ways, aren't you?' 'Huh? What?'

Your tendency to marry the wrong man doesn't help, though no woman ever does marry the right man – it takes a great deal of remodelling to make a man right, and you are often not artistic. You take longer than most to discover your disappointment – well after the children have made it impossible for you to bale out. Though as a Capricorn you find baling out impossible for the same reason as you continue to use the same annual hotel without enjoying it. Habit and fear of the unknown are stronger in you than fear of boredom and misery.

You often marry to be taken away from your present circumstances – you are susceptible to glamour, you are obedient to an earl. You want a man tender and strong, gentlemanly and chunky, a man with meat and money; a man who does what you want but a man whom you respect, one who knows instinctively when you want privacy and when you want to get busy; you want a man with quite a good degree, a man with quite a good title, a man to take you to the top of society by day and butcher you by night; a man who loves you unreservedly, like a Labrador.

It's ages before you accept the fact you can't have him. But then, you dislike doing things by halves and so you make sure that you are completely unhappy.

How Do They Put Up With You?

The major symptom of your sickness is your lack of satisfaction with any of life's gifts – always you reserve judgement, nothing ever matches expectation, there is unfailingly room for improvement, you always have something to say. You claim it is idealism, you say your standards are high, that you are ambitious, that only the very best satisfies your sense of perfection.

They say, though, your critical gifts spring from your need to have everything on your own terms; your refusal to step out of yourself, your past, your tight sense of history.

Things Capricorns Know

That religion has been responsible for more pain and suffering than anything else in the world.

Interesting Capricorn Fact

You are so mean with the heating you very often die of hypothermia.

Capricorns take heart from the fact that although dinosaurs couldn't adapt, they were the most successful species in the history of the planet.

The Capricorns

The Duke of Westminster, Duke of Devonshire, HRH The Grand Duke of Luxembourg, King Juan Carlos of Spain, Augustus John, Princess Michael of Kent, J. Arthur Rank, Idi Amin, Janet Street Porter, Shirley Bassey, Roy Hattersley, Samuel Self-Help Smiles, Howard Hughes, Matthew Arnold, Kim Philby, Ava Gardner, Princess Alexandra, Princess Alice, Noelle Gordon, Humphrey Bogart, Helena Rubinstein, Irene Handl, Denis Quilley, Louis Pasteur, Princess Yasmin, Gladstone, Peggy Ashcroft, Maurice and Robin Gibb, David Bailey, Patricia Hayes, Mike Molloy, Barry Goldwater, Richard Nixon, J. Edgar Hoover, Bernard Shrimsley, Peregrine Worsthorne, John Junor, Alexander Chancellor, P.W. Botha, Kenny Everett, Racine, Barry John, Sylvis Sims, Charles Addams, David Bowie, Graham Chapman, Roy Kinnear, Ron Moody, Wilkie Collins, Clive Dunn, Rod Stewart, Lord Acton, Alan Paton, Mick McManus, Joe Frazier, Trevor Nunn, Lord Dacre, Cliff Thorburn, Lottie Berk, Françoise Hardy, Moira Shearer, Rocco Forte, Cary Grant, Danny Kaye, Arthur Ransome, Patricia Highsmith, Richard Lester, Lord Porchester, Robert E. Lee, Liza Goddard, Federico Fellini, Puccini, HM Queen Silvia of Sweden, Simon Raven, Maggie Smith, Marianne Faithful, Magnus Pyke, Jack Lord, Sarah Miles, Ben Kingsley, Anthony Hopkins, John Denver, Jean-Pierre Rives, Colin Cowdrey, Nicholas Fairbairn, Kit Carson, Lord Annan, E.M. Forster, Andrew Cruickshank, Marlene Dietrich, Rudyard Kipling, Elizabeth Arden, Diane von Furstenberg, Joe Orton, Isaac Asimov, J.R.R. Tolkien, Ray Milland, John Thaw, Clement Attlee, Louis Braille, Sir Isaac Pitman, Sissy Spacek, Victoria Principal, Jacob Grimm, John de Lorean, Stella Gibbons, Rowan Atkinson, Phil Spector, Mao Tse Tung, Jan Leeming, Saint Bernadette, Gerald Durrell, Dennis Wheatley, Gracie Fields, Barbara Hepworth, Vidal Sassoon, Arthur Scargill, Michael Aspel, Des O'Connor, Cecil Beaton, Faye Dunaway, Aristotle Onassis, Lord Lever, Robert Service, Ethel Merman, A.A. Milne, David Bellamy, Paul Cézanne, Michael Crawford, Edgar Allan Poe, Dolly Parton, Patricia Neal, Bernard Cribbins, and Roy Plomley.

AQUARIUS

21 January – 18 February

A substantial body of research has produced evidence to suggest that Aquarians are actually a race of aliens deposited here from the first, and possibly only, joke in the solar system ('Can you see Uranus?').

If this is the dawning of the age of Aquarius (and it is) then we're in trouble. Aquarius rules bogus jokes, spurious knowledge, and the breaking down of authority into dreadfully self-satisfied, self-justifying human units. We shall be spending the next astrological epoch under the influence of Alan Alda.

Ruling Planet

Uranus rules this unfortunate sign, the planet of violent social dislocation, of wildcat strikes and unofficial stoppages, of social invention, of street demonstrations and teenage millionaires checking into the Georges Cinq. It is the sign of denim clothes and cowboy boots. Uranus is the planet responsible for call-girl chat shows, the French Revolution and four-letter television.

The absence of these disruptive qualities in the succession of Queen Elizabeth II (she was crowned under Aquarius) was the result of intensive court and diplomatic pressure against this overwhelming astrological influence. So extreme was the official censorship that it took years for Uranus to work through the system, emerging naturally enough in Aquarius with John Profumo lying to the House of Commons and the Beatles' first number one in the charts. Uranus had dealt a shattering blow at the social structure and the Aquarian Age, with all its wild, high idealism (broadly consisting of self-realization and ley lines) came tumbling through.

The Karma

The symbol for Aquarius has been interpreted as a current of water (it is the sign of the Water-Bearer, after all), or in modern times, a current of electricity. However, a growing body of opinion supports the idea that it actually symbolizes a double perimeter fence patrolled by bristling Dobermans: there is a deliberate privacy protecting the Aquarian soul, belied by the apparently open Aquarian personality. The fence is decorated with those who tried to penetrate the interior. What it is that the dogs are protecting they do not know. It's so secret you don't even know yourself. However there is enough active personality outside to keep the inside secret.

This duality occurs throughout the Aquarian experience – Aquarian socialists who own helicopters and a yacht ('I want *every*one to own a helicopter and a yacht'), Aquarian humanitarians who send their children to public schools ('Sadly I'm a greedy weakling, though I well recognize I shouldn't be'), but the explanations, though charming, are unconvincing. Other signs don't call it duality, they call it hypocrisy.

However, the attractive Aquarian principle is to scatter not hoard, to think independently, to reject authority – the Karma sends you out into the world as satirists, mavericks, madmen, pattermen, film producers, terrorists and revolutionaries (though the terror is usually exercised on your spouse, and the revolution takes place between Easter skiing and Cannes).

It is your karmic mission to come out from behind the perimeter, to involve yourself in the world, to submit to its discipline, to work through the blood and the hate and the horror, and the parking tickets, to a true hold on reality. To escape the highly coloured fantasia of life in your mind, and to batten on to actual things (income tax and VAT returns), to come to terms with the world of truck-hire, and leaseback, the world of electrical substations and towaway zones. The danger is that you see life as one large idea which you can edit at will, something you can cut and tuck, to see what the changes look like. The shock of the real world coming in can be overwhelming. Remember the central Aquarian experience was the St Valentine's Day Massacre.

The Aquarian In Society

As expected in this, the age of Aquarius, the sign is a mad fracture of talent and pseudo-talent, ambition and failure, humour and hopelessness. Pacifist Lord Soper belongs here as much as Norman Mailer, the boxing novelist. We should be not surprised to find the popular artists Neil Diamond and Desmond Morris represented. Mozart in the same sign shows how diverse the spread of talent is, as do Lord Denning and Angela Davis. John Junkin, Martin Shaw and Telly Savalas make a coherent astrological ensemble, and Nastassia Kinski with John Hurt redress the balance.

Michael Bentine is here who never made a joke that worked, Denis Nordern has never made a joke at all, but Barry Humphries has never made anything else. Larry Adler was born under this sign and brought the mouth organ to the concert hall (there was really no need to). Professor Steen Rasmussen woke up on his eighty-seventh birthday to find his intense Aquarian ambition had rewarded him with the recognition of being *an outstanding Danish townplanner*. How our spirits sink in the company of Georges Mikes and Norman Wisdom, but how they rise with Lord Byron (who like many Aquarians had such trouble with his feet).

Your high ideas (which you confuse with ideals) combining with an infantile need to test convention, lead to the most tiresome arguments in the Zodiac ('Show me from one of the four axioms of logic *why* I should not get married in my running shoes'). And you have inspired the same reaction throughout history. When the feckless Aquarian Louis XVI was guillotined in the Aquarian Revolution, the English king sent a diplomatic courier with the message to the revolutionaries finishing, 'This is not clever, or amusing, it's merely a childish attempt to shock.' Milton Schulman voices the same reaction to Aquarian theatre (*The Romans In Britain*, and all of Bertold Brecht).

Though we can recognize the basic good nature of the Aquarian, it is hard to condone the carnage you leave in your wake, as if some hungry animal had gone mad. The blood may not be on your own hands, but situations do break up behind you, under the intensity of your charismatic cross-examination (it has the force of a methedrine experience). For – like Aquarian advice columnists Claire Rayner and Evelyn Home – you appear to be vitally interested in everyone (if more in the manner of a boy detective than a sympathetic adult) and this can lead to misunderstandings (Aquarian Libby Purves is made editor of the *Tatler*).

The power of your verbal expression is remarkable. You will say *any*thing to get to know people, and in this we see your greatest, perhaps your only, charm. As if in a street fight you hit them very hard, very fast and examine them while they are still in shock. Your purpose in this is hard to deduce – it is certainly not to possess them (you aren't emotionally acquisitive, and you wouldn't know what to do with them on your mantlepiece), or to comfort them (it's none of your business, and anyway, they might want to comfort you in return which would be *sooooo* embarrassing), and certainly not, like Scorpio, to torment them ('Hey come on, steady now, settle down, okay?') Probably you just want to know a lot of people so that a lot of people know you. You don't want to be loved (this is just as well), for all that oppressive sentiment is a trap – you don't *necessarily* want to be liked, but you do want everyone to know who you are. You don't want friends, you want a reputation – what other explanation is there for Denis Skinner? Or Oliver Reed?

You Can Use People

The danger is that the objects of your examination come to think that you *like* them. They confuse your professional interest with personal good manners (not that you have much of either, but a peculiar alloy that looks like both in a certain light). The fact is you are emotionally cold. You make a superb foul-weather friend – your energies are drawn out by temporary derelicts, dock prisoners, martyrs immediately prior to their martyrdom, women at the end of their tether. As they regain normal health (or die) they lose their usefulness to you.

When you lose your address book you can't be bothered going through all the research to recompile it – you just get a new lot of friends.

This is why you raid others for their substance in a tremendous clinical coup, and leave them looted.

At your rare best you Aquarians are social vivisectionists (there hasn't been an example of this since Charles Dickens lost his talent). More commonly you will be a reckless gossip, an advanced name dropper, probably with a weight problem (like Russell Grant), though the name you drop most will be your own.

Going Home Alone

You are intensely gregarious. Your passion for company – loneliness actually frightens you (Farah Fawcett, Tallulah Bankhead) – is deeply neurotic, springing from a paranoid idea that everything is happening somewhere else. Your life is tantalized by the laughter in the next room. Everyone else, you believe, is having a much better time than you are – as indeed they probably are.

This social promiscuity will be deeply unsatisfying, leading to a loss of self-respect and eventual insanity. It is a fantasy life of contact without commitment. These 'contacts' you believe will set up like navigation lights on some social map, guiding you to the glamour that is so obviously happening somewhere. Thus you will end up a pathetic bundle on the telephone on Friday night, riffling through your address book like Aquarian Helen Gurley Brown.

Original Thinkers

You are rather proud of your originality, you present it as an attractive character strength. Because you present well, and because the times are with you (this is the dawning of the age of Aquarius), many take your word for it, forgetting that in happier times originality was something to be feared and mistrusted. Certainly your talent in this does not spring from any well of creativity, but from the fact that you cannot bear to line up with all the fat old fools who've dominated the establishment for years. This is the sign of kicking against the pricks (and you are careful to be out of range when the pricks kick back).

And You Are Necessary

In evolutionary terms, you Aquarians are society's random mutation.

Being born under this sign you will spend your lives in an often meaningless quest – for a new science of hairdressing, a new packaging technique for dandruff shampoo, a new denim look, a new way of screaming into camera, a new way of moving to the music through rush-hour traffic. Aquarians look for new, *now*, ways of doing anything there is to do (marriage, tax plans, garlic lamb), not for any value to yourselves, but because your astrology impels you to be different for society's evolutionary benefit.

Thus you are a) profoundly irresponsible, and b) generally left in some cultural cul-de-sac with an unintelligible piece of apparatus and a sense of grievance about your life.

'It isn't *fair*!' you say to your pillow. You have *lived* for others. Your vision of yourself depends on your mad belief that you are profoundly selfless, something that annoys everyone who knows you (about 200,000 people). The fact is you are only selfless in that you never let yourself be known; you are selfless in that your energy has gone into your address book and none into self-discovery (bad luck Eartha Kitt).

Apparent Longing For Universal Harmony

For someone who is so perversely original, so wilfully eccentric in the self-regarding way of a talented sixth former (you *won't* play rugby, *or* do the CCF, and you've *no* house spirit to speak of), it is surprising to find such an admiration of fraternal humanity.

Perhaps you need a neutral social element so you can easily escape through it. Your doctrinaire liberalism is keen to ignore local difference and difficulty. 'We're all just people, and all cultural codes are valid, there is no fundamental difference between different cultures,' you say in heated, meaningless arguments. Leos bluffly reply that 'Indians practise suttee, Arabs perform female circumcision, and Negroes look like chimpanzees.' You brush it under the Family of Man, admitting only when pushed that there are some *very* distant cousins out there (especially when they want to stay the night). Anything that inhibits your ability to travel pushes you back into the arms of your nearest and dearest (an appalling prospect). Harmony, order, a well-polarized element allows you a) easy passage and b) something to overthrow.

A Formidable Opponent

You have brilliant peripheral vision, like a fly. It is almost impossible to take you by surprise. You are able to talk and listen *at the same time!* This gives you an overwhelming advantage in savage arguments (see *Marriage*).

This is just as well for the survival of the sign, as the Aquarian mode of social intercourse is the argument. You love to expose the weakness, the inconsistency, the incoherence of someone else's position with your own iconoclasms. Unfortunately your lack of respect for disciplines means that you only know about things you want to know about, and this makes many of your arguments one-dimensional.

The authority for your beliefs is generally dubious, but you rarely lose an argument because you prefer meaningless statements (meaningless in Sir Karl Popper's sense of being unverifiable):

The largest ethnic minority in America is German, and this is why traffic in the States is so obedient to the speed limit.

Black holes very likely offer access into alternative universes.

The basis of structuralism's Theory of Binary Opposition has something to do with the ancient Greek practice of releasing doves from the left hand side of the mountain.

Genuinely creative people can tap into a creative plane where all media concepts already exist, and this is why whenever I write a tune, I find it turning up in a matter of weeks on Bruce Springsteen's new LP.

Highly Adept Tacticians

Aquarians set so much store on your honesty and integrity it comes as a shock to find you cheating. You will be as subtle as possible, and you wouldn't call it cheating yourself. You'd be deceived yourself by your own dazzling sidesteps, your brilliant blind-side breaks from a conversational ruck *when you haven't even got the ball!*

Such Promising Youngsters

But as you get older it is an Aquarian trait that you rarely fulfill your promise. It isn't talent that counts in the long haul, it is character – you need the character to get the talent out, and many of you are simply too fly. There comes a time when you have to stop promising and start delivering. Usually you just don't (*Who does?* you demand angrily. But you offered to, you promised to, you made everyone's life a *misery* promising to, you took out long-term loans on your exceptional promise and suddenly it's time to pay and you can't even calculate the interest – no good at maths – let alone deliver on the principal – and you who are always so strict about debt!)

Great Rapport With The Mentally Ill

You take patently absurd ideas seriously – as a liberal you don't care about people, you care about principles, much as mad people do. You have a lot in common with the insane, so you talk to them seriously, not to help them, but to be in on the action, to be along for the ride, confident you can bale out when the fuel's gone.

You have a lot of faith, too much hope, but no charity at all.

Statistically, Aquarians are over-represented in mental hospitals and psychiatric wards. More Aquarians work for J. Walter Thompson than any other advertising agency. You respond well to electric therapy (much as Aquarian Gary Gilmore would have done if they'd given him the chance).

Health

Though some Aquarians are teetotal (the sign of the genuine

alcoholic), most Aquarians drink too much ('Fuck my liver before it fucks me,' as one New Zealand Aquarian puts it). Yet you are cranky about your diet. Though you will scoff down doughnuts and fastfurters during the day, you insist on lo-cholesterol brancakes for your breakfast. On balance you eat badly, and your autopsy will reveal five pounds of undigested red meat in your lower bowel.

Highly strung, nervous, sociable Aquarians are victims of Filofax fever.

You are often clinically mad and not susceptible to treatment.

In The Late Twentieth Century

Other signs should be careful of identifying Aquarians too closely with the late 1960s. It is by no means a sign devoted to communes and cannabis resin: the same high-school Aquarians who featured at Woodstock discovered cocaine in 1977, and were very shortly cramming the polls in 1980 to vote in their fellow Aquarian (the third Aquarian President of the US).

A clockwork Messiah, you have been called, 'Wind him up and he saves the world.' You do suffer from a passionate belief in causes, and this can confuse those around you. They may mistakenly believe you to be ready to support your violent rhetoric with some action, or at least some money. However the violence of the Aquarian Age is largely performed by other signs (Aries, Taurus, Sagittarius, Leo) though with the blessing of all Aquarians who like to see formal order destabilized. A Taurean in the White House would be very dangerous.

Group endeavours will be encouraged, and this can be good, paradoxically, for the bourgeois individualist.

Your Career

You will achieve prominence, success and respect, but not

much (Ronald Reagan is the best example of this). Many Aquarians peak too early (Christopher Hampton) while others don't peak at all (Raymond Baxter).

Success is immensely attractive to you, you want it, you want it badly. Your democratic approach to better men than yourself ('They put their trousers on same as me, one leg at a time') may disguise this, but you are fatally attracted to the glamour of the brand-name rich. Of course you cultivate poor people too (it's no fun being rich if everyone's rich – the pleasure in having money lies in seeing students standing at the back of the auditorium, seeing civil servants in the stand-by queue at Heathrow, seeing wage-earners in the three-day line for Debenham's sale – you may even stop to chat democratically, and to rub it inconspicuously in).

However, you are hindered in a commercial career by your distaste for chasing after money – you find it undignified. But your objective interest in people offers you a fine career in marketing providing you don't have to start door-to-door (your feet will quickly turn on you). You also overspend splendidly, and this causes considerable anxiety to your financial planners, your tax collector, and of course to yourself. It does, however, keep you working, and you are a good, if unreliable employee. You make a dreadful employer though. The responsibility appalls you – the lack of company at the top is frightening.

But what a fine corporate whore you make, and you cheerfully acknowledge this in job interviews (often including the interviewer in the analysis ('We've both been round the block a couple of times, right?'), and this is one of the few things that has a morbid effect on your career (that and your body-bruising hangovers).

As a corporate whore you have no beliefs, but you do have opinions about everything, and this is useful in business meetings where the last one on his feet talking is the winner. Your opposition may suspect you have been abusing cocaine, and in extreme cases they may lay anonymous information with the relevant authorities.

Aquarian Product Ideas

Personal stereo headphones with a pilot-style microphone attached to allow the consumer to sing along with the music directly into his own ears.

Retractable bayonet directional indicators for bicycles – they sit in the hollow handlegrips and shoot out, for roundabout work.

A signal tower of variegated plastic to sit in the middle of fast-food restaurant tables – flashing bulbs indicate More Coffee – Bill Please – Come Here Quickly – Hey, Isn't It A Beautiful Day?

'And even if we only achieve a *fraction* of these projected sales we'll still make a million,' you tell your friends. You tell them this with such energy you have none left to pick up the phone and dial a designer.

Romantically, Men

You are a big wet dog, with the emphasis on dog.

Your ordinary social mode is mistaken for more interest than you feel. You come into the bend far too quickly saying anything you can to make contact – 'Who is this strange young man?' older women will wonder, and smile in spite of themselves.

You don't fear intimacy, but you aren't really very interested in it, something many women find dangerously exciting. Your Aquarian personality is rather chilling, too, the distance, the brio, speed. Imagine trying to get close to Aquarian Bamber Gascoigne?

You like the idea of love, partly because everybody else does. Everyone you admire in the great gay world has love affairs so you do too. It's how you meet new people; they remember you because you make them fall in love with you. This is attractive of you. However, your tactics are better than your strategy, and you frequently get lost in your short term love affairs (the sense of direction is bad).

You may also answer your domestic telephone with the words 'Mission Control', and many women cannot take it.

But So Constant

Despite the sudden and alarming dislocations in your personality, there are two statements you invariably make: 1) I'm not ready for a commitment, and 2) I'd like us always to be friends.

In Love

You can't say 'I love you' quietly and neutrally, as though you mean it. You say '*Jesus* I love you, I really do, it's incredible to me this feeling that I have for you, how amazing it is, I've known nothing like it before in my life.'

Somehow the conversation always comes back to you.

Sexually

Physically you are somehow ill at ease, despite your cowboy boots and the circuit training. You are not sensual; you sense no mystery in the flesh. The only mystery for you is why others make so much of it. Conquest has its pleasures, however, but only once. And maybe once again, a week later. You get to the same point in a relationship then you bale out. You haven't had many sexual experiences, but you have had the same experience many times.

It can be an appalling trauma for you, nothing like you expected. Your Mental – Air approach does little to prepare you for the tears and the sweat and the blood of sex, the fumbling buttons and sudden embarrassing noises, the strange birdlike cries in the back of the throat, the mute resentment following your incompetent crisis.

Physical sex drains you, evacuates your spirits, emphasizes your separateness, your loneliness. It takes the glow of the dream away and leaves you with raw flesh in the overhead lighting. You prefer the endless possibilities of a fantasy world, and indeed Aquarians do make the best pornographers.

But you want to talk about it excitedly with your friends. You're good at the looking part of it too, you have a fine, level stare. But when it actually comes to clambering over the front seat of your Bentley to get at the Australian au-pair cowering in the back, your courage fails you ('What if she starts screaming? Didn't you see a policeman coming?') It is fantasy that appeals to you therefore, and you live a lot in the half-light, with invisible moves and a deep touch that seems to go down like hands in a hot pool.

This is why you want to do things that are impossible; you want to bite off an ear lobe and stick it back with saliva; to massage her stomach from the inside, up to the elbow in her intestine; you want to spin together on your sexual axis and play your guitar in time to it. You are wholly unequipped for such adventures, except in your head.

Maritally

You are intensely unfaithful and perhaps it's just as well. You are no good at love. Sex and romance you can just manage, though intermittently and for the conversation it generates. You need something to keep you going, and though your appetite is easily satisfied at any one sitting, you are soon hungry again.

As the marital trap clangs behind you there is a sudden sense of all the girls out there with whom you haven't slept, and it is unbearable. You look over your shoulder as you walk back down the aisle and you see all those girls moving to the music, in their unbearably short dresses, and the way the brown hair on their forearms catches the light is unbearable, and it's unbearable how their breasts move in their shirts, and the way their collars come edging up into the soft part of their throats is unbearable.

But you have to be married as you take a lot of looking after. It works as an institution should. The objective sense you bring to the relationship is useful particularly for keeping the partner at a distance. However, your need to uncover things which are hidden (an Aquarian compulsion) will lead to tears and violence. Opening Pandora's box did no good to anyone, least of all Pandora. But because you don't have the imagination, charity or strength of character to lie, you insist on regular declarations of guilt with self-abuse and self-abasement. It's a form of egotism.

You are not suited to marriage at first, and throughout the early years you continue to wipe your greasy fingers on the curtains.

Women

For all your airiness of manner you are a fixed sign, and obduracy, obstinacy, and implacable bloody-mindedness are your major characteristics. That and a voice like a car crash. You have quite a lot of self-control which you apply – sometimes viciously – to parts of your personality while other parts are in uproar, and this is your most amusing characteristic. From the way you talk you seem to have recently been in an explosion. You also lack the apparatus for proper honesty, and substitute outstanding frankness instead. This makes a mess of those around you. You also have opinions about practically everything, and a dangerous sense of being responsible for everything, which leads to guilt and anxiety. When enjoined to think before you speak you often say, 'How do I know what I think till I see what I say?' The fact that this first appeared in the mouth of a cartoon five-year-old does not stop you saying it well into your forties.

Despite the emphasis you place on friends, the clashing

plaids of your personality make intercourse with you very difficult, especially social, spiritual or commercial. Your bruising frankness doesn't help either ('No, darling, it isn't very big at *all*, I'm used to much larger ones than that'). You have the talent for opening old wounds, but lack the touch for healing them over.

There is a sense of absent-mindedness about you too, when you can't talk your attention wanders. The fact is you have no natural manners, and no interest in others: you question them rarely, and only as a form of self-examination. You never ask a question without knowing the answer, and often you play both sides of the conversational net – 'It's more efficient that way.' It can be a surprise to find radical lack of confidence in this extroverted sign. Your lack of insight into your own character often degrades you into a creature of doubt and indecision, making abstract thought impossible. What passes for thought is merely your larynx vibrating in tune with your subconscious. Thus you make yourself vulnerable to cold, clever men. Though your total recall and motor mouth are more than adequate defences against criticism (you *will not* be criticized).

Sexually, Women

You have mixed feelings about men (scorn mixed with anger), and you are not well-equipped to make the best of a situation, and curiously inert when it comes to the flesh, curiously without confidence. You are not passionate, except in your opinions. Alert to criticism, alert to looking foolish, there is something innocent about you which no amount of sex will touch. You live more and more behind the perimeter fence, and the dogs make it as hard for you to get out as for others to get in.

You use sex not for itself, nor even for food, but as evidence that you are liked. You cannot be told often enough how likeable you are. When you cannot find sex you build your inability into a general theory of abstinence (see Germaine Greer).

But unlike other signs you can recreate yourself in the night and awake as though you hadn't been touched, and this makes men fall in love with you. Perhaps it doesn't lead to happiness, but you never really expect to be happy, and this is your greatest talent.

The Aquarians

Telly Savalas, Martin Shaw, Benny Hill, Denis Nordern, Jimmy Tarbuck, Frank Muir, Dora Bryan, Ned Sherrin, John Junkin, Oliver Reed, Prunella Gee, Larry Adler, Lee Marvin, Roberta Flack, Greg Norman, Mark Spitz, Earl of Stockton, Robert Wagner, Joyce Grenfell, Bertolt Brecht, Jimmy Durante, Ian Gow, Georges Simenon, Barry Humphries, Gene Pitney, Thomas Malthus, Helen Gurley Brown, Sir Arthur Bryant, Len Deighton, Milos Forman, Jack Palance, John Travolta, Jocelyn Stevens, Frank Harris, Alex Comfort, Havelock Ellis, Sir Max Aitken, Claire Bloom, Georges Mikes, Jane Seymour, Galileo, Peter Adamson, John McEnroe, Alan Bates, Mary Quant, Burt Reynolds, Lord Boothby, Paul Hamlyn, Anthony Howard, Zeffirelli, Marie Lloyd, Kim Novak, Janet Suzman, Mrs Patrick Cambell, Ronald Colman, Peter Jay, Charles Dickens, François Truffaut, Patrick McNee, Jack Nicklaus, Placido Domingo, Paul Scofield, Laurence Whistler, John Hurt, Nyree Dawn Porter, Lord Byron, D.W. Griffith, HRH the Grand Duchess of Luxembourg, HRH Princess Caroline of Monaco, Bill Gibb, Lord Denning, Jeanne Moreau, Stendahl, Ernest Borgnine, Neil Diamond, Lord Duncan Sandys, Bamber Gascoigne, Nastassia Kinski, Desmond Morris, Earl Spencer, Ann Todd, Hadrian, Raymond Baxter, Somerset Maugham, Virginia Woolf, Marquis of Bath, Michael Bentine, Marti Caine, Jack de Manio, Jacqueline du Pre, Jules Feiffer, Christopher Hampton, Eartha Kitt, Paul Newman, Baroness Maria von Trapp, Douglas McArthur, Ronald Reagan, Alan Alda and the first television broadcast, William Randolph Hearst, the deaths, on the same day, of Randolph and Winston Churchill, Jerome Kern, Mikhail Baryshnikov, Acker Bilk, James Callaghan, Alfred Marks, Ronnie Scott, Gordon of Khartoum, Colette, Jackson Pollock,

Germaine Greer, Tony Blackburn, Victor Mature, Viscount Tonypandy, W.C. Fields, Sir Fred Catherwood, Gene Hackman, Viscount Long, Lord Lowry, Hal Prince, John Profumo, Vanessa Redgrave, Boris Spassky, Percy Thrower, Carol Channing, Christopher Chataway, Norman Mailer, Jean Simons, Lord Soper, Dame Freya Stark, Zane Grey, Tallulah Bankhead, Terry Jones, Sir Stanley Matthews, Sir John Nott, Muriel Spark, Peter Tapsell, Clark Gable, S.J. Perelman, Les Dawson, Farrah Fawcett, Norman Fowler, Valerie Giscard d'Estaing, Hughie Green, Libby Purves, Elaine Stritch, Nell Gwynne, Val Doonican, James Michener, Doris Speed, Frankie Vaughan, Walter Bagehot, Hylda Baker, Norman Wisdom, Charles Lindbergh and Susan Hill.

PISCES

19 February – 19 March

Your symbol puzzles astrologers. What does it mean? It is a diagram of contrary impulses pulling in two directions (Harold Wilson and Lady Falkender)? Or is one sinking (Mary Jo Kopechne) and one swimming (Teddy Kennedy)? Are they two fish dinners? A sexual position? or an exciting new packaging technique for off-the-bone tuna? Only the Piscean knows.

Pisces is the symbol of unification. Of holistic philosophy. of astrology, and psychic surgery, of belief in Tarot, telepathy, the prophecies of Nostradamus and the Bermuda Triangle. It's the end of the astrological cycle – necessarily, because things just couldn't get any worse.

The Karma

You have worked long and hard through the twelve school terms of the Zodiac and here, in your Oxbridge year you have privileges which you frequently ignore or abuse. The Piscean philosopher Schopenhauer illustrated this profound astrological truth by developing a theory to demonstrate that will was more important than knowledge – *the exact opposite* of what Pisceans believe. Such characteristic perversity deals a significant blow against those who would wish to discredit astrology.

Your Piscean mission is to transcend the physical, to rise out of your body, like an angel, and exist in the clear world which you glimpse (according to the ancient art of numerology) between the third and fourth sip of your second cocktail.

Pisces is the sign of the self-undoer. Your deep need is to be reintegrated with the universe, to be spread across the cosmos like margarine. You want to let the dykes of your personality break down, to dissolve the constructs of self and society. To let the jungle in. To let the tide in. You want radiation to wash through your nerve circuitry. You want to plug into the universal grid. You want to see X-rays. You want to join in the dance of energy and matter, in the interstices of time and space.

Well, you *can't*.

Your spiritual maturity, the deepest in the Zodiac, leaves you unimpressed with the world and its rewards. It is significant that the one Marx Brother born under this sign was *Zeppo*.

The Peculiarity of the Fishbrain

Some people need to be taken out of themselves. You need to be put back. Cardinal Newman was an example of the extra-cranial Piscean.

You can have very peculiar ideas about the world, believing that God was a spaceman, or that He wears skirts and carries a crook. Anything is possible for you. When you open up the top of your cerebral cortex, nothing is refused entry.

You attempt communication with plants, dolphins, prostitutes. You are a huge, equal-opportunity receiver, accepting calls in heroic confusion. *The Dukes of Hazzard* intercut with *Open University*, minicab shortwave and bleeper signals for doctors on duty. You give it all equal weight – witchcraft, extra terrestrial civilizations, the synchronicity of tea leaves, ley lines, pendulum dowsing, pyramid wisdom, astral travel, spoon bending, Keynsian economics, out of the body experiences, Rocky Horror philosophy, nothing excites you more than anything else. With your mind on eternal verities you sense an underlying futility in conventional ambition – causes don't appeal to you, nor do prospects of horror move you.

But you want to understand about everything. *'Liberal!'* they jeer at you, and they are right. Like liberals, deep down, *you don't care*. You want everyone to have enough so that you need not feel guilty. You want to be left alone to consider your own predicament, your place in the psychic universe, and this is confused by the structure of your mind.

You do not live in the left hemisphere of your brain, in the logical, literate, masculine side; nor do you live in the right hemisphere, the intuitive, visual, femine side.

You live on the Bridge of Sighs that connects them.

The traffic on the bridge is absorbing. Especially the man dressed in a cloak of shadows who swoops over you in the night, and takes you away in his darkness.

Characteristic Piscean Types

A certain sort of comedian was born under this sign: Frankie Howard and Kenneth Williams. Bruce Forsyth and Tommy Cooper. Bernard Bresslaw. But then both Lord and Lady Baden-Powell were also born *on precisely the same day*, in this sign. Patrick Moore, the skeptical astronomer, demonstrates the Piscean proclivity for getting very fat. Lord Snowdon demonstrates the Piscean's sometimes unhealthy preoccupation with the sick and Sir Robert Mark demonstrates the utterly un-Piscean qualities of policemanlike authority –the famous 'wild card' we so often find in members of this sign.

Your Planet

Neptune is the ruler of Pisces and represents deception and chaos. It is the planet of uncut hallucinogens and certain types of fungus; it rules quantum mechanics, probability theory, late arrivals and multiple pile-ups on motorways. It was the planet of bad influences when you were young (Catholic boys in wind cheaters with Swiss knives) and has grown up with you.

As the King of the Submarine World in classical mythology, Neptune, your ruling symbol, offers an insight into the intuitions of the first element of the world. There are deep channels of communication of which normal people know little.

Neptune is the source of disease and incurable lunacy, of degrading drinking, and lapping at cocktail waitresses, and orgies and perversions and flickering your tongue at pleasant women in the street. However it has a persuasive quality too, and your attorney can often plea-bargain down from guilty of common assault to guilty of being under the influence of Neptune (the sentences are rarely custodial, much as you need it).

Some Astro-Social Facts For The Eggheads

Neptune was discovered in 1846 – only *three years after hypnotism* was first discovered, and *barely two years* before the year of revolutions in Europe – a year which historians now agree was a crucial catalyst in the development of Western civilization.

However it was a year of unprecedented peace, clarity and stability in China, which is clearly part of the reason why astrology is still so different in the East – ex oriente semper aliquid novum.

The Piscean Personality

Secretive but open, cruel but kind, nasty but nice, sadder but wiser, you Pisceans have the dual nature which (so the skeptics say) astrologers can make mean anything. However, we can say without fear of contradiction, there is no doubt that both Johnny Cash and Caruso were born under Pisces.

There may be a strong sense of swimming both ways about

you, but it generally operates on the principle of improving your bargaining base in every situation – thus, you are possessive but promiscuous, loving but loose, deceitful about little things (calorie intake) but open about others (systematic sexual infidelity).

You need the best of both worlds, and you've developed an ethical system to allow this. The fluid world you live in doesn't have either/or choices. Questions that have yes/no answers bewilder you, they don't make any sense, you hear the words but you don't know what they mean. Thus you move in and out of situations without making any impression on them – not because you're indecisive but because you feel any decision is misleading. Your fish face in opposite directions, and for either to swim away would not be helpful. This is what you tell your credit managers, and you get some rather old fashioned looks.

Your short-term memory is not good, and honesty is often the only policy possible.

Big Dreamboat

Your personality looks best under low lighting; your pale colouring comes into its own under a sort of submarine glow; nights suit you better than days, as you drift around smoothly and easily. The night is a submarine element through which you drift with others of your kind. When the world is sleeping your sensitive mind picks up messages, information – the sort of information that is useless to normal people (that's why they're asleep) though a clever, disciplined, determined Piscean (nine of these exist in Britain) can – improbably – make a lot of money from it. So alone in the Zodiac you are not afraid of the hour before dawn when the night seems it's been going on forever and will never end. However, this strength and these hours make you eccentric: you care so little what society thinks that you may still have a lava lamp in your bedroom.

You are the spinners of dreams, you live with shadows and fantasms. You can get lost in dreams of love, or money, or great success – you need help to drag you back into the real world of

PAYE and tow-away zones. However beguiling the world of the mind you must keep up the payments on your car. Your mind exists for a foot from the side of your head, and it changes colour with your moods.

The bailiffs, the repossession agents will be impressed with this, but not moved.

Physically

You often have big, bulging eyes, like a semitic blowfish. You also suffer from bad feet. Billy Beaumont, who captained England for a record 21 rugby internationals had trouble with his feet. It was the least of his troubles. You wake up slowly, if at all, and even then you exist in a world of whales singing and radiation dance. Moods flow across your face like wind on a wheatfield, and this can frighten those who don't know you. Those of you who learnt this lesson keep all facial changes subcutaneous – Patrick McGoohan has dominated 1,200 hours of television with a range of just two expressions (asleep and camera-ready). Many Pisceans suffer from a difficult birth (you are aware of what's ahead, and you don't like it), and in extreme cases you suffer from brain damage (sometimes parents never find out).

You are delicate but can astonish medical science with your powers of recovery. You are often afraid of ageing and dying – again, you know what happens on the other side, and it is not a pretty story.

You Can Be Rich

Especially if you inherit. Pisceans can have a character flaw which generally prevents them making money. Whereas Aries make venture capital prospectuses, and Capricorns make a steady twelve per cent on capital, you Pisceans tend to make cheeseburgers in a theme restaurant.

However, your unworldliness can be an advantage in your

formative years, plugging you into an intuitive network of trade information, predicting commercial trends, political movements, merchandising opportunities. The best examples are Sir James Goldsmith and Rupert Murdoch. The worst examples are William Davis and Gyles Brandreth. George Harrison as an example is neither one thing nor the other – very Piscean. However, the principle of Pisceans dreaming their way to success obtains only past a certain point in your capital formation. Remember that as a water sign your liquidity must be high, your cash-flow must be strong, and your fixed assets secure. Only you know how unlikely this is.

As a Piscean you are severely astrologically handicapped. Your gentleness, sensitivity and imagination are said to justify the raft of indolent confusion you float around on but they don't. Your reputation for being hopeless with money, however, is more than justified. You're not even very good with restaurant bills – 'Yeah, look, we don't actually have any *money* right? But we've got this amazing idea for a cartoon strip . . .'

The number of Pisceans lying – *at this very moment* – on Indian-print bedspreads looking at the day-glo poster of Jimi Hendrix is as large as the population of Nigeria.

It is sobering to realize that the Chancellor of the Exchequer is Piscean.

Your Career

You are low on the food chain.

The negative capability which you have in generous amounts suits you for any job where you have to take on someone else's identity: acting, writing, marketing, submissive spouse.

You are very schedule D – the restrictions of office life grate. You operate best as a commission artist, on the royalty turnout. Tap dancing on the tube, or busking Shakespearian monologues, or break dancing in Covent Garden for provincial tourists (you can leap four feet in the air and land directly on your forehead) are all traditional Piscean occupations. You need your own private space, and income. You should avoid jobs where willpower or rational thought is needed, or standing out in the cold. You drift in and out of jobs, affairs, banks, prison. You know the shadowplay for what it is, and you take nothing very seriously. You are keen not to discuss money, and you are often left with the bill. When you die your family may discover a sofa under a pile of your unopened bank statements.

You suffer from vocation. The Piscean affinity with the feet can lead you into chiropody, or door-to-door selling, or ballet dancing (Rudolf Nureyev was born under this sign). Social work is attractive to you, if to no one else you know, and the Caring Society (1968–79) was your natural habitat. Your cover was finally cleared off by thirty per cent inflation, the fall of the last Labour Government, and the Falklands War.

All you really want to do is sit with a gin and watch gravel gardens being raked.

Perverted Pisceans

However when you repress your astrology you can turn the other way. In terminal cases the Piscean may turn himself into a caricature of his opposite as a hard, grasping, domineering, manipulative bug-eyed bastard. Inverted Pisceans are the most dangerous astrological type in the Zodiac. They have the skills of Scorpio in their deep strategies, but a random element in their makeup gives them a rogue strength (this is Rupert Murdoch). No contract is too strong for them to break, no agreement so secure that they cannot turn it to their advantage. They are a pleasure only for other Pisceans to work for.

In The Media World

You make dreadful film producers. Instead of shouting at people, like Leos '*Work Harder and Faster for Less Money!*' you slide around: 'Hey we're working for a larger issue all right?

The point is to see all that money up on the *screen*, right, guys? Don't we?'

However, your abilities in deep strategy suit you for work in the upper management, out of the hurly, out of the world. Robert Altman, often one of the best directors in the world, made less money from *MASH* than his son did (his son wrote the song). However, neither of them made as much out of it as Alan Alda, the awful Aquarian entrepreneur.

As a Piscean performer you suit self-crucifixion, alone in the spotlight, *suffering* in front of your public. Your taste for drinking a very great deal of alcohol encourages popular opinion to distinguish you as an artist.

You Believe In

Astrology, numerology, horology, tarot, psychic surgery, Time travel, that whales sing to each other from 20,000 leagues under the sea, that Kennedy was killed by Texan oil interests, Kirlian photography, reincarnation, Nostradamus, pyramid power, the Lost Continent of Atlantis, that Pepsi Cola financed the invasion of Afghanistan, that Mayans were performing open-heart surgery 3,000 years ago, aura analysis, communication with chlorophyll, spiritualism, vegetarianism, Hinduism, Woodstock, I Ching, UFOs, palmistry, phrenology, poltergeists, ectoplastic manifestations, and that Paul McCartney actually did die and was only partially revived.

Drawn To The Unknowable

Psychos, psychics, psychiatrists, physicists and artists. Alone in the Zodiac you have a real chance of looking beyond the daily grind in the crush bar, to look up and out at what it is that is casting the shadows that constitute the material universe. You believe that your body is a three-dimensional shadow cast on four-dimensional space-time by a five-dimensional super being. Or possibly more than one being, in possibly more than five dimensions. Anything is possible for the Piscean.

Piscean Science

Your intuitions about the deep structure of the world offer blinding and often incomprehensible insights. Sub-atomic particles disappear here and reappear there without passing through any intermediate points in this dimension. This does not worry you. It might be an electron travelling forward in space, or it might be a positron travelling backwards in time. Either is acceptable to you. So are cheeseburgers.

Your yes/no switches do not work. Everything depends. Like electrons, you exist in a probability cloud. Your close relationships with members of the opposite sex are subject to Heisenberg's uncertainty principle: this suggests that the more you know about a particle's velocity the less you know about its location. You know everything about where it's going but nothing about where it is. The more you know about one of these things the less you know about the other. In your love affairs you are acutely aware of the strengths of your relationship, but you have no idea where you'll be in three months time. Or you may be determined that in three months time you'll be in New York but absolutely no idea who you'll be when you get there.

However, Einstein was a Piscean and he didn't believe in quantum mechanics.

But Nonetheless You Can Be Gullible

Irish women come up to you in the street and say they've just got out of a mental home and can you spare something to help with their train fare home because they've been robbed. 'You poor thing! My uncle was in a mental home for a time too! Which mental home was yours?' They can't tell you. 'What was the matter with you?' They can't tell you that either. You reason they were being treated for amnesia. 'God, how *awful*!' You give them five pounds. 'You couldn't make it ten, could you sor?'

You are the derelict's best friend. You fall for the shy, the sick, the shop-soiled. You love people for their bruises. As their wounds heal, you lose interest. When the mad old women wail at you in the street, you don't react angrily. You beam at old men with their overcoats tied up with string, migrants looking for work with all their possessions in a carrier bag. Your heart swells for harp seals, beagles with emphysema, Ethiopian babies. You feel so sorry for them you can marry any one of them. You are natural drug addicts, and this can spill over into your social and intimate relationships.

In Love

However, you are good at love, seeing it and finding it everywhere. You may be short, but dwarf love is the strongest. When thrown over by someone you love the pain is intense and may destabilize your never-very-steady emotions. But you also metabolize grief quickly, often in minutes, and such an ability eases your passage through multiple partners, as Piscean Rex Harrison's 27 wives will testify (as indeed they did testify). This can cause pain to those who are in love with you, but your charm is immense and you don't really care. Like Aquarians, you are exceptional hypocrites, and much of your talk about cosmic consciousness is because you don't want to do the cooking.

Driving

You often drive very slowly and aggressively, scowling over the wheel; or else fluidly and freely, in and out of breathtakingly dangerous situations (you believe you will never die).

Your short term memory is such that you regularly forget

where you parked the car. Sometimes you return by public transport forgetting that you took the car at all.

In fog you are carriers of the infection medical science knows as motorway madness.

Sexually, Men

Sex with the fish can swing both ways.

On days of anxiety and high achievement (bad days) you Pisceans go looking for a way out of this world on to a higher plane. You will not be deceived by the illusion of sex. Like Hindus you fear a woman's sex as the organ of Maya, and you enter her as though entering a grave.

No matter how undressed you may become you can never be completely naked, always covered by some secret, some richly coloured, highly worked fantasy. Sex with you is a mental experience; they enter with you into some psychic community. Currents flow out of you and swaddle your partner. You can touch her (if it is a her) everywhere at once, she feels you inside and outside, diving into her declivities before and behind. When you are relaxed, confident, harmoniously tuned (better days, they happen regularly, twice a year) your fluid intuition can allow a fine interpenetrative experience. As a Neptune ruled sign you excel in diving. You can embrace her with your limber fins, and she likes you for it; you can surround her all by yourself. This happens on the sofa (she never quite knows how you do it, and she complains afterwards about the dry cleaning on her loose covers), or more conventionally in bed over the weekend. Here she complains you make her late for work as she loses track of time, and is woken by the alarm on Tuesday.

This fluid nature helps a great deal on the early dates when you can get your hands inside her sweater without her even noticing. By the time you have infiltrated her brassiere she is already breathing heavily and her protests carry no authority. You can go on to stop every orifice of her body (including her nostrils) with your all-pervasive personality.

It is the Piscean talent to change shape in a series of slow dissolves, langorously, amorously. Your body twists and thickens, you can invade your partner's person from unexpected angles, your fluid nature seeps into her porous flesh: a woman finds this strangely exciting. She will open out to you, and you can see down into the darkness at the bottom of her brain, where whale backs break out into the moonlight, rising and shining black on the surface, sounding down into the deeper darkness. They are never quite sure what they have on their hands, and until they find out, the thrill of romance is overwhelming.

Pisceans make fine pan-sexual beings. You do not submit to the draconian laws forbidding free passage, free trade, free intercourse – as a citizen of the sexual world you have visas for every known country and permanent residence in many of them. You are not subject to genital fascism, and often claim to make love with the whole body (especially when impotent). But at least you don't both hobble to work the next day, with aching organs.

Parentally

Your abilities are not the highest, in spite of your deep intuitions. In America more Piscean parents are sued by their children for negligence and malpractice than any other sign. A Piscean couple in San Diego, California displayed such a casual attitude to family law they were successfully sued by their Aquarian Cabbage Patch (TM) Kid for the net value of their joint pension.

Women

Pisceans are the embodiment of all we used to call eternally feminine – frivolous, unpredictable, limber, clingy, cute and great in bed. You are interested in shoes, and over-running your credit limit. You are long-suffering, and bitterly sarcastic. You like to wear big fluffy sweaters and to put others before yourself. You can create cosy, calm, homely havens of tranquillity by sucking all the chaos out of the room and ingesting it. It's a valuable trick, but it plays hell with your internal structure and your autopsy reveals that you are riddled with chaos. It's often a contributory cause of death.

But suffering is what you do best, and this is why you want to do all the suffering yourself you cannot bear to see others in pain, you want all the pain for yourself, if for nothing else than to reinforce your rather mature attitude to the universe: 'Life is such a bitch,' you say, 'it's amazing we get out of it alive.' You say this partly because you have no brains at all, and partly because it's true.

Your nature is such that men feel they can ask you to wear crotchless panties for easier access. You will poutingly acquiesce. But they shouldn't be deceived, because your submission will probably be tactical: deep in your satirical soul you are – incredibly – the most independent sign of the Zodiac. This makes your pose of Helpless Woman profoundly deceptive – though strikingly effective. The Helpless Woman is making a come-back, though exactly why strict fiscal policy should be so interlinked with sexual ineptitude, astrologers no less than economic scientists are unable to say.

But faced with a Piscean woman dressed in silk, in a dress that falls down her back like water, men, grudgingly, will forgo their feminist sympathies.

Some Say You Need Help

Your emotions are confused, like a fig basket full of adders. You are inclined to make the same mistakes again and again, partly because your ideas change, and partly because practice makes perfect.

It is important for you to choose the wrong lovers, to practise your gifts of sacrifice and renunciation of the devil, the flesh, the world. Perhaps this is why you take so many drugs, or abuse alcohol with that steady, professional rate of take. You are trying to equalize the pressure inside and out: when you are full, you can swim out of the air-lock into the submarine landscape where the strange fish are.

So though you are always available, you are always elusive. So much so that many think you are a slut. You go out for cigarettes and they never see you again. At your funeral, your many lovers – unaware of each other until now – get on rather well for a while ('What on earth did she see in *him*?' each will ask himself later). You certainly soak up a lot of different experiences in life from many types and conditions of men (your mother would *die* if she knew). You can be dissociated though, so much so that you can hide from a headache in another part of your head.

When you are loved you actually change colour, and this makes men *nervous*. No one can keep it up, the input schedule is too demanding.

Your Relationships

In your generally unsatisfactory affairs you find it impossible to find total support. But then you are not looking for a man so much as an exo-skeleton into which you can pour your fluid self to achieve form and permanence.

You will do anything, yes *any*thing, for this, and sensing your desperation men will fuck and run. Though, worse, others stay for years. There is a sly look about you which inflames a certain sort of man; there is much of the minx about you. Also men have the sensation that you would do for them the things they would never dare ask anyone else to do. You do, too, and this contributes again to your talent for suffering.

But things are always going wrong, and it must have an effect on what modern technical experts call your mental health. The karma is too hard for your human half, and it may generate a lot of *anger*. You should be careful that this doesn't have the effect of hovelling you in tight inside yourself.

You can be aware of the pain of life without being deceived by it. You may be unhappy, but then who isn't? Your life may be a mess, but then everyone's is. There are very few things that matter: men, money, and God are the only things that matter, those are the only things that make you whole. And blinds too, nice blinds are imporant. Men, money, God and nice Austrian blinds, and a good laundry service, and a video, and a telephone machine that says you're out even when you're not, and a big sofa from Conran costing over £900, and a Bentley. And men, that's right. And God.

In The Late Twentieth Century, Men and Women

Your spirits flicker in the shadow of the bomb; the confusion of international markets, drought and low harvests make you anxious. Love comes and goes; relationships are overfreighted and fail; the weather changes, the news carries stories of violence and counter-violence. Try to salvage something from the slaughterhouse. They are hosing down the killing yards for the day, and the weather is changing.

The Pisceans

Patty Hearst, Robert Altman, Cecil King, Humphrey Berkeley, Nina Simone, Jilly Cooper, Douglas Bader, Edward Kennedy, Christine Keeler, Frankie Howerd, Bernard Bresslaw, Kenneth Williams, Tommy Cooper, Bruce Forsyth, Niki Lauda, Richard Goolden, Cardinal Newman, Duchess of Kent, Sheila Hancock, Sir John Mills, Schopenhauer, Anthony Burgess, George Harrison, Tom Courtnay, *Zeppo* Marx, Mohammad Ali, Fats Domino, Rex Harrison, Peter Carter-Ruck, Barry Fantoni, Sir David Beattie, Harry Belafonte, Roger Daltrey, Andrew Faulds, Lytton Strachey, Sandie Shaw, Lawrence Durrell, Joanne Woodward, Ralph Nader, Lord and Lady Baden Powell, Anton Mosiman, Dennis Waterman, Peter Fonda, Betty Marsden, Renoir, John Arlott, Caruso, Sir James Goldsmith, Rupert Murdock, Fanny Craddock, William Cody, Elizabeth Taylor, Joan Bennett, Lord Cowdray, Johnny Cash, Harry H. Corbett,

Rossini, Chopin, Glenn Miller, David Niven, Doris Hare, Pat Arrowsmith, Jean Metcalfe, Jean Harlow, Ronald Searle, Patrick Moore, Vivaldi, Peter Skellern, Lord Beveridge, Ring Lardner, Lord Snowdon, Cyd Charisse, Lynn Redgrave, Kenneth Graham, Peter Quennell, Bix Beiderbecke, Prince Edward, James Herriot, Rupert Murdoch, Liza Minelli, Max Wall, L. Ron Hubbard, Jim Slater, Albert Einstein, Mrs Beeton, Pam Ayres, Jasper Carrot, Lord Melbourne, Patricia Nixon, Leo McKern, Rudolph Nureyev, Robin Knox Johnson, John Silkin, John Updike, Sir Richard Burton, Dr Livingstone, Ursula Andress, J.P.R. Williams, Professor Eysenck, Andy Gibb, Samantha Eggar, William Davis, Dame Kiri Te Kanawa, Gyles Brandreth, Ivan Lendl, Sir Ranulph Twistleton-Wykenham-Fiennes, Jocelyn Hambro, Piers Paul Read, Viv Richards, Earl of Snowdon, Douglas Hurd, Bill Beaumont, Bobby Fischer, Lady Falkender, Sir Michael Havers, Nigel Lawson, Harold Wilson, Edward Albee, Dr Giovanni Agnelli, Andrew Young, Terence Brady, Joe Bugner, Sir Robert Mark, Michael Caine, Alan Hare, Sir Hugh Walpole, Lord Marsh, Rita Tushingham, John Wain, Ry Cooder, The Ides of March, Bertolucci, Jerry Lewis, Kate Nelligan, George Ohm, Patrick Duffy, Hurricane Higgins, Kenny Lynch, Patrick McGoohan, Brian Clough, Roger Whittaker, Albert Chevalier and Michael Heseltine.

Fritz Spiegl
Keep Taking the Tabloids £1.75

Exclusive – Spiegl On the Street! Meaning a survey by Fritz Spiegl of the contribution to contemporary popular culture made by the denizens of Fleet Street. *Keep Taking the Tabloids* shows the World According to the Hacks. A place where everyone not *hitting out* is *appealing*, where price increases are *slapped on* to make *costs soar*, where every ambulance is making a *mercy dash* and every inflamed chip pan is a *fire drama. Vice probe horror shock – bishop named* is an effective way to sell papers. So that's the way the industry is run. Now in these *exclusive and revealing* pages Spiegl shows you how it's done . . .

Fritz Spiegl
Dead Funny £1.50

'Beneath this sod lies another' – the long-awaited sequel to *A Small Book of Grave Humour* from the ever-watchful Spiegl who, during the years of success of his first collection of the funnier side of tombstones, has continued to collect mirthful *mementos mori.* He has now put together a second book which promises to be every bit as popular as the first.

Peter Mayle and Gray Jolliffe
Man's Best Friend £3.50

Over the years man has achieved many things. Yet he has never quite come to terms with the constant companion in his trousers. He humours it when it behaves badly, forgives it when it doesn't behave at all. It is lazy, demanding, socially unreliable and selfish. By rights it should be outlawed from polite society. Short of surgery there seems no hope of improvement – perhaps the worst is yet to come.

Peter Mayle and Gray Jolliffe
Twinkle Winkle £3.50

Here it is – 'man's best friend' and the stars – the world's first guide to below the belt astrology. Taking the twelve signs of the Zodiac, this book goes where no book has gone before in revealing the mysterious effects that the date of birth has on Wicked Willie's comings and goings. Throw away your crystal balls! *Twinkle Winkle* is all you need to find out what fate has in store, and how much trouble it's going to get you into.

Juliet Sharman-Burke

The Complete Book of Tarot £2.50

Tarot cards are like mirrors which reflect unsuspected knowledge deep in the unconscious mind. This teach-yourself guide to reading the cards is designed to help activate and stimulate your innate sensitivity as a first step in developing intuition – the hallmark of the serious Tarot reader. Whether you want to interpret the cards for others, or use them to help gain a much deeper and more revealing understanding of yourself, you will find *The Complete Book of Tarot* both instructive and inspiring.

Shirlee Kiley and Rochelle Gordon

Your Name is Your Destiny £1.50

The complete guide to understanding and analysing your name. Learn how to discover its meaning and discover your fate, your future and your fortune. Discover the key to the characters of your friends, lovers, children. How changing your name can change your life, transform your destiny and fulfil your greatest potential.